MW00929486

Inspiring Stories for Amazing 8-Year-Old Girls

Motivational Book about Courage, Confidence, and Kindness: Uplifting Stories Empowering Inner Strength, Honesty, and Friendship (for Young Readers)

Jenny Aster

Contents

Introduction

Welcome to "Inspiring Stories for Amazing 8-Year-Old Girls" — a book that celebrates the unique potential within every girl.

Imagine waking up each day feeling powerful, fearless, and ready to embark on any adventure. Sounds thrilling, right? That's exactly what every girl can achieve with the right inspiration and mindset.

This isn't just a collection of stories; it's like a super special box full of fun, engaging tales that take you on a journey through challenges and triumphs. Each story is designed to teach valuable lessons about confidence, self-love, and the importance of kindness. Have you ever felt a bit unsure or wondered if you could be as brave as you dream? You're not alone! Confidence is a skill, like riding a bike or mastering your favorite game, and it's something you can learn and grow.

Meet girls just like you in each story, discovering their own strengths and realizing it's perfectly okay to feel uncertain at times. Through their adventures, you'll learn that a little courage and a lot of fun can help you uncover your true potential. Plus, every chapter ends with a special message, summarizing the lessons learned and encouraging you to apply them in your own life.

Parents, prepare to witness the remarkable growth your young reader will experience through these stories. This book is crafted to be more than just enjoyable reading—it's a powerful tool to help your child develop the skills and mindset they need for a confident, fulfilling life.

Embark on this exciting adventure and discover the greatness within. Enjoy reading and exploring the incredible stories that await you!

Your journey to confidence and courage starts here.

Have fun reading!

Copyright © 2024 by Jenny Aster

All rights reserved.

No part of this publication may be reproduced, distributed, or transmitted in any form or by any means, including photocopying, recording, or other electronic or mechanical methods, without the prior written permission of the publisher, except as permitted by U.S. copyright law. For permission requests, contact [include publisher/author contact info].

The story, all names, characters, and incidents portrayed in this production are fictitious. No identification with actual persons (living or deceased), places, buildings, and products is intended or should be inferred.

ISBN: 9798333151353 (hardcover)
ISBN: 9798332250637 (paperback)

The First edition of 2024

CHAPTER 1

Learning to Love Who I Am

It's the start of a new school year, and I'm happy and a little scared. As I stand in front of my mirror, trying to fix my curly hair, I can't help but feel nervous. I should be excited. But all I can think about is my wild, bouncy, curly hair. It won't do what I want.

"Why can't my hair be simple like Sophia's?" I sigh, looking at myself in the mirror.

Sophia's hair is straight, like a calm lake. But my hair? It's curly and wild, like a river that can't stay still! I try to push my curly hair down, but the curls bounce back like they're playing a game. It feels like I'm the only one with such silly, bouncy hair!

At breakfast, I couldn't stop frowning. "What's wrong, sweetie?" Mom asked, seeing my sad face.

"It's my hair," I mumbled, poking at my cereal. "It's all... curly. Why can't it be nice and straight like Sophia's? She looks so pretty."

"Oh, Daisy," Mom said softly. "Your curls are beautiful. They're part of what makes you, you! Sophia is lovely, but so are you."

"Really?" I asked, looking up at her.

"Really," she smiled, hugging me. "Everyone's different, and that's what makes us all special."

I tried to listen to Mom. She said it's cool to be unique. But inside my head, a little voice kept whispering, 'I don't want to be different. I wish my hair were straight like Sophia's.' Then, I wouldn't feel left out when other girls talk about their hair.

I picked up my backpack and felt a bit sad. I tried to remember Mom's words about being unique. But, sometimes, it's tough to believe.

On my way to school, I whispered to my curls, "Let's be friends today. No jumping." I imagined my curls nodding and settling down to behave.

A Big Announcement

"Hey, do you see Mrs. Parker's sparkling eyes?" Sophia whispered. Giggles filled our classroom. It was bright and full of colorful posters.

"What do you think it means?" I whispered back.

Mrs. Parker clapped her hands and grinned wide. "Guess what, class?" she said, her voice bubbling with excitement. "I have a surprise for you today!"

Sophia and I exchanged curious glances, our minds racing with guesses. What could it be?

With a dramatic pause that made everyone lean in closer, Mrs. Parker announced, "Next month, we're going to have a play!"

The room burst into loud cheers and claps. Everyone around me was jumping up and down, super excited.

Sophia turned to me, her eyes big and sparkly. "Daisy, isn't this awesome? What do you think the play will be about?"

I nodded, feeling my heart pounding fast. "Yeah, it sounds fun," I managed to say, but my voice was quiet.

I looked at my reflection in the window. My hair was everywhere, like a crazy crown. "But what role could I get with hair like mine?" I wondered,

Around me, everyone was shouting their guesses.

"Maybe it's about space aliens!" yelled one of my classmates, his arms zooming like a spaceship.

"Or maybe a story about magic and wizards!" another guessed, waving her arms like she was casting a spell.

Over in the corner, some kids were buzzing about the play. "I'm gonna be the star!" one said, beaming.

"And I'll be the sneaky villain!" another chimed in, making us all giggle.

I watched, tilting my head. They all seemed confident and eager. Then, I whispered to Sophia, "Do they have a worry-off switch? How can they be so sure?"

Sophia giggled. "Maybe they drink superhero juice for breakfast!"

I scratched my head. I was pretending to search for a confidence button on myself. "Maybe my switch is stuck," I said with a funny face.

Sophia laughed and nudged me. "Or maybe we just need to find where they hide that superhero juice!"

"Yeah, or some magic confidence glitter or something!" I added, and we both burst into giggles. Imagine ourselves sprinkling glitter all over before stepping onto the stage. Suddenly, my mind started to swim with scary thoughts.

"What if I forget what to say during the play? What if everyone laughs at me? What if my curls go wild under the bright lights?" Each worry made my heart beat fast. It felt like I was running a race. With every doubt, my dream of acting in the play started to fade.

Mrs. Parker notices everything. She saw me fiddling with my hair and being extra quiet, so she came over with her warm smile.

"Hey, Daisy," she said gently, sitting down next to me. "You seem a bit quiet about the play. Is everything okay?"

I shrugged, a little shocked that Mrs. Parker had noticed how quiet I was. "I'm just...nervous, I guess. I wish I looked like anybody else." I mumbled.

Mrs. Parker leaned in close, lowering her voice like she was about to share a big secret. "You know, I used to worry about standing out because of my glasses. Thought they made me look too different," she said with a chuckle, tapping the frame of her glasses. "But then I realized what makes us different makes us special. Like your awesome curls! They're what make you special and unique, and they help show who you are. Who knows? They might just be the star of the show!"

I blinked, surprised but feeling a tiny bit better. Mrs. Parker always knew what to say.

"Picture this: You find a beautiful flower blooming in a garden. It catches your eye. It stands out from the other flowers' vibrant colors and unique shapes. Like that amazing flower, you are also unique and special! You have your own special qualities and talents that make you who you are."

Sophia, who had been listening, jumped in with a big smile. "Yeah, Daisy! Your curls are like your superhero cape. Just imagine them sparkling under the stage lights!"

Those nice words about my curls being like a superhero cape made me smile. "Maybe being different isn't so bad," I thought, but I still wasn't sure. Inside, I felt a mix of happy and worry.

"Are you going to try out for the play?" Sophia asked as we walked down the hallway.

"Maybe I'll try," I said, my voice shaky. I'm nervous but want to see if I can do it."

"That's so brave of you, Daisy! What if you get a big part?" Ellie piped up, her eyes wide with excitement.

"That's not going to happen," I replied, and we laughed.

And I said, "Even if I don't get in, at least I'll have tried, right?"

"Exactly!" Sophia encouraged. "And we'll be there to cheer you on. You're going to be great!"

I nodded, feeling a tiny bit braver with my friends by my side. "Audition day, here I come," I whispered to myself as we stepped out of the school, the idea slowly settling in.

The afternoon sun peeked through the clouds as I walked home from school. It cast long shadows on the pavement. "Hey, Mr. Sun, is that a good sign?" I whispered, seeking comfort.

The sun beamed warmly. "I'll take that as a yes!" I whispered, trying to build my confidence.

Just then, Sophia rushed around the corner, her face a mix of excitement and nerves. "Daisy, you look like you're thinking hard!"

"Yeah, you know.... Am I the only person this nervous?" I confessed, my stomach doing flips.

"No, me too! I'm pretty scared and can't stop thinking about it," Sophia said, chewing on her lip. "But we can be nervous together, right? And support each other?"

"Absolutely! We'll help each other!" I managed a shaky smile and gave her a high five.

Audition Day

In the bathroom this morning, I stared at my reflection and whispered, "You can do it, Daisy." My curls bounced as if they agreed.

On the way to school, Sophia skipped up next to me, her face all lit up with excitement. "You're going to be awesome, Daisy!" she cheered, her smile bright as the morning sun.

I giggled, feeling a little better but still wishy-washy inside. "I wish I could borrow some of your confidence," I said, half-hoping she had some extra stashed away.

"Don't worry, Daisy! I'll be cheering the loudest for you," Sophia promised, quickly hugging me. "We'll both do great!"

Her words made me feel a little braver.
Together, we walked the rest of the way to school.
We were ready for the auditions.

At school, the time finally came for the audition.

"Okay, everyone. Remember that you all are
special and unique. Embrace your uniqueness.
Appreciate the things that make you who you are."

"Whenever you're ready, Daisy," Mrs. Parker
said. She gave me a reassuring smile as I stepped
onto the stage.

I gulped, looking out at the chairs with students.
"Pretend they're all my cuddly toys," I whispered,
trying to steady my wobbly legs.

"You can do it, Daisy!" whispered Ellie
from behind the curtain, her voice full of
encouragement.

"Okay," I took a deep breath. "Here I go."

"Just like in rehearsal, you've got this," Mrs. Parker encouraged gently, nodding at me to start.

I took a big, deep breath and started saying my lines. With each word, I felt my voice get stronger. "I can do this," I told myself, picturing my cuddly toys nodding along.

When I finished, Mrs. Parker clapped and beamed at me. "Good job, Daisy!"

When I was about to step off the stage, Sophia came bouncing up "You did it, Daisy! How do you feel?"

With a big smile, I said, "I'm glad it's over, but I feel really happy!"

Sophia high-fived me, and we giggled. I was super happy I made it through.

A Surprise Turn

When the cast list finally appeared on the bulletin board, my heart raced as I spotted my name at the very top.

"Me?" I gasped aloud, my eyes wide as I stared at the paper. "But... what if I get too scared with everyone watching?"

Sophia squeezed my shoulder, smiling big. "You'll be amazing, Daisy. Just wait and see."

Then, I heard some whispers behind us. "Daisy got the main part? Really?" one of the kids muttered, sounding super surprised. Another added, "I didn't think she'd get the lead."

Sophia turned slightly, her eyes sharp. "Hey, why don't you watch her first before you say things like that?" she said, standing up tall.

I felt a big knot in my throat, but Sophia wasn't having any of it. "Daisy worked really hard for this. Just watch, she'll surprise everyone," she insisted.

The whispering stopped, and I felt a little better. I hoped to be as brave as Sophia believed I could be.

Feeling the tension, Mrs. Parker approached us, her expression concerned. "Is everything okay here, girls?"

Sophia nodded. "We're fine, Mrs. Parker. Just talking about the play." As Mrs. Parker walked away, Sophia leaned in close to me. "Ignore them, Daisy. They're just jealous. You earned this part, and you're going to be fantastic, I know it!"

Their words stung a little, and I chewed on my lip, imagining a sea of doubtful eyes all over me.

Practice was hard work, but it was more challenging with those doubts echoing in my head. But night after night, as I rehearsed my lines and songs, I whispered to myself, "I got this."

One evening, while I was practicing in my room, my brother popped his head in and grinned. "Hey, are you training to be a superstar or something?"

"Hope so!" I giggled, shuffling my script.

He stepped inside, pretending to bow deeply. "Well then, I must get your autograph now, future star, before you're too famous!"

"Only if you promise to save me some cookies from the jar!" I shot back.

"Deal!" he laughed. "Just don't forget your biggest fan when you're a celebrity!"

"I won't." We chuckled.

The Night of the Show

Finally, it was THE night. Backstage, I felt my heart doing a jumping jack inside my chest. I sneaked a peek at the crowd through the curtains. "Look at all those faces," I whispered to Sophia, both of us peeking at the audience.

Then, I remembered something really important, something my mom told me: "Your uniqueness is your magic." She also told me that when I have a negative thought, I should change it into a positive one. I should focus on things I can do. Those words made me feel a bit braver. So I repeated, "I got this, I can do this, I can handle my curls because it's me." And then, somehow, I felt more confident.

I took a deep breath, hugged Sophia quickly, and entered the spotlight. It was showtime.

As I spoke my last line, I felt really good, like everything was just right. "Wow, this feels right," I thought, the words coming out smoothly.

From the side of the stage, Mrs. Parker gave me a big thumbs-up and said, "You're doing great!"

As soon as I finished, everyone started clapping loudly. It sounded like thunder!

Sophia rushed over to me as I walked off the stage. She gave me the biggest hug ever.

"You were super awesome, Daisy!" she said, her eyes sparkling like tiny stars.

Mrs. Parker came over with a huge smile. "Daisy, you were wonderful! You were a true star tonight."

Sophia bounced up beside us, grinning from ear to ear. "She's right, Daisy! You were amazing!" I felt like I had done something really special. I faced my fears, showed everyone the real me, and had so much fun doing it.

"I did it," I thought, standing tall and proud. "I was just me—curly hair, big laughs, and all—and it was perfect."

That night wasn't just the end of the play; it felt like the beginning of something new for me. Being different is cool. With my head up high and my curls bouncing, I felt ready for whatever comes next. I felt like I could do anything!

Daisy's Lesson:

I learned something really special: It's okay to be different. My curly hair and big laugh make me, me! I don't need to be like Sophia or anyone else; I just need to be myself. I found out the magic wasn't somewhere out there—it was inside me the whole time, and that's pretty awesome!

Message to you from Daisy:

"Remember, you're awesome just the way you are. Never forget that the real magic is being yourself." Love, Daisy

CHAPTER 2

Tides of Friendship

"Hey, what's this?" I called out.

My voice bubbled with excitement as I brushed away the sand.

My friends huddled close. They narrowed their eyes as they looked at what I had found.

"What did you find, Skylar?" Ethan asked, tilting his head to get a better look.

"It's a bottle!" I said, holding up a glass bottle. "I can see something in there, but it's all cloudy!" I squinted, trying to see through it.

Kylie leaned in, her nose nearly touching the bottle. "It looks mysterious. What do you think it is?" she whispered; her eyes wide with wonder.

"Maybe it's a secret message," Anna suggested. Her imagination was already dancing with possibilities.

"Or a treasure map!" Liam added, his voice cracking with excitement as he jumped a little.

"Let's open it and find out!" Ethan said, clapping his hands together eagerly.

The friends nodded. Their faces lit up with curiosity. They were ready to discover the secrets of the foggy bottle.

The Sealed Message

"Can I open it, please?" Kylie's eyes lit up with excitement as she reached for the bottle in my hand.

"Be careful with it!" I cautioned her. Then, I handed the mysterious bottle to Kylie.

Kylie nodded seriously. She carefully twisted the rusty cap. "I wonder what secrets it's hiding," she whispered, her eyes focused.

As she finally popped the cap off. A musty smell of old seawater wafted out. Ethan scrunched up his face. "Ew, it smells like old socks!" he exclaimed, but he kept his eyes glued to the opening of the bottle.

Kylie tilted the bottle. A tightly rolled piece of paper edged out. Before Kylie could take it, Ethan quickly grabbed it from her. His hands shook a bit with excitement. "Got it!"

"Hey, I was supposed to do that!" Kylie said with a frown, sounding frustrated as she looked at Ethan.

"It's a map!" Ethan announced, unrolling the paper on a flat part of our beach blanket. The paper was old and a bit torn, but a big, red X stood out clearly. "Look, there's an X right here! It must be a treasure map!"

"A treasure map? For real?" Anna gasped, leaning over the map alongside the rest of us.

Liam began bouncing around us. He chanted, "Treasure map! Treasure map!"

I grinned at my friends, swept up in the thrill of it all. "Imagine what could be there! Maybe it's not just gold or jewels—what if it's something that nobody has ever seen before?"

"Yeah, let's be treasure hunters!" Ethan cheered, high-fiving Liam.

With the map and our imaginations running wild, we were ready for an adventure.

The Journey Begins

"Let's find out what's at the X!" Liam shouted, his eyes wide with a mix of thrill and a tiny bit of fear.

"Yeah, this is so exciting... but also kinda scary," I admitted, feeling my heartbeat faster. "We've never found anything like this bottle before. What if we find a real treasure or stumble upon a secret pirate hideout?"

"Or maybe there are clues and puzzles we've never seen!" Ethan said, his voice shaky with a blend of nervousness and excitement.

Kylie held her beach hat tightly, nodding. "It's like we're real explorers. But it's a bit scary stepping into an adventure like this."

Anna clapped her hands, but her smile wavered a bit. "It could be something amazing, or something else...I don't know!"

The beach had always been our playground, full of fun and games. But today, we had the mysterious map. It felt different. It felt like the start of something unknown and a bit scary.

"Wait, look at the back of the map!" Liam exclaimed. We all leaned in close. We tried hard to read the tricky words.

"This clue is hard," Anna said, scratching her head. "It says, 'Where waves meet sand and seagulls land, look below where little shells stand.'"

"What does that even mean?" Ethan frowned, looking puzzled.

"It sounds like a beach riddle!" I suggested. "Maybe it's near the shoreline where the seagulls hang out?"

"Yeah, and maybe 'little shells' means we should look for a spot with many shells!" Kylie added, her eyes lighting up.

"We can figure this out together!" Anna's voice was full of determination now.

We all nodded. We started walking along the water's edge, looking for any odd pile of shells.

"Over here!" Liam suddenly shouted. He was pointing at a cluster of small shells arranged oddly in a circle. "This has to be it!"

We rushed over and began to dig carefully in the sand beneath the shells. Working together, we moved sand and pebbles, and our hearts raced with excitement.

"Anything yet?" I asked, wiping sweat from my forehead.

"Not yet, but keep digging!" Ethan encouraged, feeling a mix of nerves and excitement as we dug deeper.

The clue had brought us this far, and I felt we were on the edge of solving something big.

Teamwork or Trouble?

"Look what I found!" Ethan shouted. He held up a small, waterproof container. We all crowded around. We were excited. But, as he opened it, our excitement turned to curiosity. He revealed another clue.

"Read it, Ethan! What does it say?" Anna bounced on her toes, trying to catch a glimpse.

Ethan unrolled the paper. His brow furrowed as he read, "Beneath the guardian of the shore. There, wooden sentinels watch the sea. Find me where children play, and shadows lay."

"I don't get it," Kylie frowned, scratching her head. "What's that even supposed to mean?"

"It's talking about the old dock. You know, where the wooden posts stand like guards?" Liam suggested, his voice filled with hope.

"That doesn't make any sense! It's not even close to where kids play!" Ethan snapped, ignoring the idea quickly.

Kylie's face flushed red with frustration. "Well, do you have a better idea, Ethan?"

"Yeah, Ethan, you don't have to talk that way," I said. I could feel the tension rising among us like a tide.

"I'm just guessing here!" Ethan shot back, sounding a lot sharper than before.

The arguing got out of control. Each of us shared our thoughts. But nobody listened to each other. It felt like our fun adventure was turning into a real mess.

"Guys, stop!" I finally shouted, louder than I intended. Everyone fell silent, looking at me. "Let's listen to each other's ideas," I suggested, my voice softer. "We're friends. We're supposed to work together, not fight."

Making Peace

The beach was very quiet except for the sound of the waves. We all looked at each other, our anger fading as we realized how silly we were being.

"It's okay to be frustrated," I reassured them. I felt the need to keep us together. "But let's remember why we're here. To have fun and find the treasure."

Ethan lowered his eyes, kicking at the sand. "I'm sorry, guys. I didn't mean to be so bossy."

"And I'm sorry for snapping," Kylie added, her voice softening. "Maybe we can check near the old dock and along the beach. Families love picnics there. That could be 'where children play,' right?"

"That sounds like a plan," Liam agreed, the first to smile again.

"Yeah, let's do that. And we can enjoy the beach a bit," Anna suggested. She hoped to lift everyone's spirits.

As we walked toward the old dock, the mood lightened. We talked and laughed. We remembered that the treasure hunt was supposed to be fun, not a battleground.

The Unexpected Twist

As we got closer to where the map showed the final clue, I stepped on something hard. "Ouch!" I yelped, jumping back. A big crab in the sand was waving its claws in the air.

"It's as scared as we are!" Anna said, seeing its beady eyes dart around. "Let's be careful and help it move away."

Ethan knelt down slowly, using a stick to guide the crab toward a safer spot gently. "There you go, Mr. Crab. No need to be scared of us," Ethan said. Then, we all laughed.

The last clue was under the old pier. It was dark and echoed, making our voices spooky.

"I'm scared," Kylie whispered, her voice shaky.

"We'll be brave together," I said, squeezing her hand. We all held hands and felt stronger.

"Let's find that clue," Liam said. Then, we stepped into the shadowy space by the giant rocks.

We found the spot on the map by the giant rocks, but the big crab was there again next to the rusty box.

"Maybe it wants something?" I guessed, noticing how it watched us.

"Let's try giving it some seaweed," Anna smiled. We found some nearby and offered it to the crab. It grabbed the seaweed. Then, it started munching.

"Sometimes, we just need to understand," I said with a smile. We reached for the box. The crab no longer minds us.

Treasure and Promises

Inside the rusty box, we found old coins, each one different. Some were shiny, and some were green like the sea.

"Look at this one! It's got a ship on it!" Kylie exclaimed, holding up a shiny silver coin.

"Yeah, and this one's got a funny face on it," Ethan laughed, showing us a green coin.

We also found notes folded up like secret messages. Liam picked up one and read, "This treasure brought us here. But friendship kept us together. Share kindness like it's your treasure."

"Here's another one," Anna said, unfolding a yellowed paper. "It says, 'Every friend is a new door to a different world. Open it with care and joy.'"

I found a note with a drawing of four kids smiling. "Listen to this," I said, reading aloud, "'We found this treasure on a sunny day, just like you, and you did a great job finding our notes! Understanding each other is the real treasure. Pass it on.'"

"We're part of a big adventure story, just like them!" Liam said, his eyes shining.

Their Mark

Feeling inspired, we decided to add our note. "Let's write something cool for the next kids," I suggested.

"Yeah, about friendship and having fun together!" Kylie added.

Anna went home and got a piece of paper. We all wrote together. We said, "Today, we learned about friendship. Being kind and understanding each other. They make everything better." We each drew a little picture—a star, a wave, a sun, and a smiling crab.

"We'll put this with the other notes," Ethan said, carefully placing our message in the box.

Goodbyes

In the late afternoon, we dug a spot to bury the treasure.

I said with a grin, looking at my friends, 'Today wasn't about finding treasure.' It felt more like a secret mission to learn about each other. And you know what? "Our friends are the best treasure we have!"

"Yeah, the best friends and the best day ever!" Liam cheered.

"We'll come back one day," Kylie promised, patting the sand over the buried box.

We left the beach with our hearts full of happy memories. Our adventure had brought us closer than ever.

Skylar's lesson:

Skylar learned that feeling what others feel—like when you know a friend is sad or happy—is called "empathy." It's a big word that means caring about others' feelings. She learned that working together and caring for each other can turn tricky times into great adventures and help everyone grow closer.

Message to you from Skylar:

"Hi! Did you know that understanding others' feelings, or empathy, can help solve problems and make adventures more fun? The coolest thing I found out is that the best treasure isn't gold or jewels—it's the strong friendships we make. Always remember, being a great friend is the most valuable treasure!"   Love, Skylar

CHAPTER 3

Bravery in the Night

I'm Avery. I'm eight years old and have a huge imagination and a big secret. I'm scared of the dark, especially when it's time to sleep. My mom tells me, "All kids get scared sometimes." But I feel a bit silly about it. "Big girls like me shouldn't be scared of the dark," I whisper to my stuffed bear, Cuddly, when no one else can hear.

In my room, I try lots of things to keep the bad dreams away. I count sheep, but they won't jump over the fence in my head. I drink warm milk, but it doesn't help. I even listen to calm music, but the scary dreams still sneak in. I look up at my glow-in-the-dark stars, but they don't do much. "Why do I have scary dreams when other kids get fun ones?" I think, feeling all alone.

"One night without scary dreams, please," I whispered to Cuddly.

"I feel sad. It's like I'm the only one who gets scared." I hugged Cuddly closer and whispered again, "I don't know if I can face the nightmares. They're just too frightening." Cuddly looked at me with his sweet smile and listened quietly.

Just then, my mom peeked into my room. "Sweetie, why are you still awake?" she asked as she sat beside me on the bed.

I looked up at my mom, my eyes big and worried. "Mom, I'm scared of having bad dreams again," I told her, holding Cuddly even tighter.

My mom wrapped her arm around me, pulling me close. "It's okay to be scared, Avery. Everyone has bad dreams sometimes, even grown-ups. But remember, those dreams can't hurt you. They're just stories your mind makes up while you sleep," she explained softly.

"Can Cuddly and you keep the bad dreams away?"

"Of course, we can try," Mom smiled, kissing my forehead.

"How about we keep Cuddly right here next to you, and I'll check on you during the night? We'll both make sure you're safe."

"Thanks, Mom. And thank you, Cuddly," I said, giving my stuffed animal a big, grateful squeeze.

As my mom turned off the light, I felt a bit braver with Cuddly by my side. Knowing my mom was just down the hall, I closed my eyes, ready to try to sleep, feeling less alone with my fear.

As I lay in bed for a while, I saw something strange. In the corner of my room, where my toy box usually is, there was a tiny door glowing softly. "Cuddly, look!" I whispered, forgetting about my fear for a  moment and filled with wonder. "Was that door always there?"

I stared at the tiny door in my room, glowing softly. "Do you see that, Cuddly?" I whispered, feeling both thrilled and a hint of fear at the same time.

The doorknob was so shiny and golden that it sparkled like magic. It made me think of going on big adventures.

Holding Cuddly even closer, I tiptoed to the door, my heart beating fast like a drum.

"Should we open it?" I asked Cuddly, looking into his button eyes for an answer. I felt scared because opening a door to somewhere unknown was a big deal. "What if it's a door to somewhere amazing?" I thought.

Standing in front of the door, I hesitated for a moment. "What if something scary is on the other side?" I worried. But, I was also very, very curious.

Gently, I touched the doorknob. It felt cool and smooth under my fingers like it was asking me to turn it. I took a deep breath and slowly turned the doorknob, half expecting something to jump at me.

But I couldn't believe my eyes when the door swung open quietly. There wasn't a scary monster or a dark closet on the other side. Instead, what I saw were beautiful, swirling colors. The stars twinkled even brighter than any I had ever seen from my window at night.

"Wow," I gasped. "It's like stepping into a rainbow," I exclaimed, amazed at the beautiful sight in front of me.

I stood at the doorway, holding Cuddly tight and feeling unsure. In front of me was a world like a dream, with a soft twilight sky and dreams flowing like a stream. It was so beautiful, like a storybook come to life. Taking a deep breath, I stepped in, even though I was nervous and unsure.

"Hello, Avery! Welcome!" a gentle voice called out. I turned around and saw a kind-looking creature with a smile that felt like a warm hug.

"I'm the Dream Guardian," the creature said. "I've been waiting to meet you."

The Guardian looked magical, glowing softly and making the air shimmer like morning dew. They changed shape like clouds on a sunny day, but their smile was always clear and comforting. It made me feel safe and loved.

"Now, let's take a journey through this land of dreams. You'll see how magical it can be.

I felt very excited with Cuddly in one arm.

With the Dream Guardian leading the way, I started my adventure. The land was filled with places that looked a little spooky at first: huge mountains that reached the clouds, wide rivers that roared, and a dark forest that looked like it had secrets.

The Mountain of Doubts

"Wow, it's so big," I said, staring at the huge Mountain of Doubts.

The Dream Guardian smiled. "Yes, it is. But do you know a secret? Each step you take makes it smaller."

"How?"

"Like this," the Guardian encouraged. Together, we took one step, and then another. After a few steps, I stumbled.

"I can't... It's too hard. My legs feel heavy," I said, discouraged.

"Hey, Avery," Cuddly seemed to whisper, "remember when you thought you couldn't finish that big puzzle? But you did, piece by piece."

"Okay, one more step," I decided. And with each step, I felt stronger, the mountain becoming just a hill.

After we climbed and climbed, I couldn't believe we finally made it. I stopped and looked all around. The Mountain of Doubts wasn't a big scary mountain anymore; it was just a little hill under my feet! I turned to the Dream Guardian with a big smile.

"We did it! It's just a hill now!" I said, feeling super happy and proud. We climbed all the way up, and it wasn't so scary.

The Dream Guardian nodded, their smile as warm as ever. "You see, Avery, every challenge seems big at first. But with courage and small steps, you can overcome anything."

I looked down at the hill we just climbed and then at Cuddly. "I guess I was braver than I thought. It was like doing a puzzle, just one piece at a time."

"That's right," the Dream Guardian said with a smile. "It's not about never being scared or doubtful. It's about facing those feelings and moving forward."

As we kept walking through Dreamland, I started to feel a lot better. The mountains didn't seem so scary anymore, and my worries felt lighter. With my friend Cuddly and the Dream Guardian's wisdom, I felt ready for anything.

The River of Fears

Next, we reached the River of Fears. The rushing water made my heart race. "I can't do this. It's too scary. The water moves too fast!"

The Dream Guardian pointed to some big stones in the water. "These are stepping stones of courage. Your fear will diminish with each step you take."

I stood in front of the rushing River of Fears. Stepping stones were there to help me cross. But they looked small.

I wasn't sure I could make it across.

I looked at the Dream Guardian, who always helped me when I was scared. Then, I looked down at Cuddly, my stuffed friend. It seemed like Cuddly was nodding, saying, "You can do it, Avery!"

Taking a deep breath, I stepped onto the first stone. Whoa, it wobbled a bit under my foot, and my heart jumped. "Oh, be careful," I whispered to myself.

I knew I had to be brave. I told myself one step at a time, ready to keep going.

Keeping my eyes on the next rock, I took another careful step. This rock didn't wobble, and I breathed out a little sigh. "Okay, we can do this, one rock at a time." I felt a little stronger with each word.

"Look, Cuddly, we're almost there!" I whispered to my stuffed bear, amazed at how far we'd come. The river that had looked so frightening before was just steps to hop across now.

When I stepped onto the last rock, I stopped and looked back to see all the rocks we had crossed. "We did it, Cuddly! We really did it!" I cheered, hugging him tight, super proud and happy.

When I finally stepped off the last stone and onto the safe ground, I couldn't believe it. I was very scared at first. I moved slowly and was super careful with each step. But I kept going. And now, here I was, standing on the other side of the River of Fears

The Forest of Shadows

Standing at the edge of the Forest of Shadows, I felt a flutter in my tummy. The shadows moved around like they were playing a game, whispering secret things. Holding Cuddly, I looked at all the dark and light playing hide and seek.

"This looks spooky," I said, trying to sound brave, but my voice shook slightly. Cuddly seemed to agree as he wiggled a little.

"It does," the Dream Guardian said, nodding. "But remember, every shadow has a story. Maybe they're just waiting for someone to listen."

I glanced at Cuddly, then back at the Guardian. "What if they're trying to tell us something fun?" I asked with a smile.

"Exactly! Let's find out. Say hello," the Guardian encouraged with a gentle smile.

I took a deep breath and shouted, "Hi, Shadows! I'm Avery, and this is Cuddly." It felt like the whole forest moved closer to listen. Then, I heard a soft whispering coming back, just like a secret being passed around.

I giggled and said, "They sound like they're playing a game, just like when I play hide-and-seek with my friends." It made me feel like the trees and shadows were not so scary after all; they were just playing their own fun games.

As I walked out of the forest, I felt proud. "I was scared, but I talked to the Shadows—with my Cuddly right by my side—and guess what? The Shadows were actually pretty nice! They weren't trying to scare me; they were just being shadows," I said, starting to understand everything better.

I turned to the Dream Guardian, my eyes all shiny with excitement. "I learned something super awesome today. When I'm scared, I can talk to what's scaring me, and maybe it'll turn out to be something really cool."

"That's exactly how you find bravery," the Dream Guardian said, nodding at me.

Hugging Cuddly tight, I felt I could do anything. "Next time I get scared, I'll think about the Forest of Shadows and how Cuddly and I made friends with the shadows.

As the Dream Guardian's voice faded, everything around me slowly disappeared. The tall, spooky trees from the Forest of Shadows became pretty patterns on my bedroom walls.

I was back in my cozy bed, holding Cuddly just like in my dream. My adventure had taken me to some amazing places, but now, all tucked into bed, I felt safe and brave. The shadows in my room didn't scare me anymore; they seemed like friends, smiling. I snuggled deeper into my blankets, excited for my next dream adventure, knowing I was braver than ever.

Avery's lesson

Avery learned that it's okay to feel scared sometimes. It's part of growing up. Now, when it's bedtime, she is not scared at all. She knows that even if she has a nightmare, it's just another adventure waiting for her. Dreams can be exciting and fun.

Message to you from Avery:

"Bravery is like saying 'hello' to your fears. Every great adventure starts with courage, even when you feel nervous. Remember, being brave helps you do amazing things!" Love, Avery

CHAPTER 4

The Power to Speak Up

"I can't believe those girls are being so mean to me. I wish I knew how to stand up for myself," Ava said softly to herself.

Ava's Struggle

Why does speaking up have to be so scary? I sat under the big oak tree at the playground. I held my favorite book tightly and watched the other kids run and play.

Just then, Ben came over, swinging his folded umbrella by his side. "Hey Ava, why are you sitting here all alone?"

My heartbeat was fast, and I stared at my shoes. "I wish I could just hide," I whispered. "Why do you want to hide?" Ben asked, looking concerned.

"It's Emily and her friends," I said quietly. "They keep teasing me."

"That's not nice," Ben replied softly. "Did you tell a teacher?" I moved my head from side to side, and my hair swung in front of my face. "What if they tease me more?"

Ben thought for a moment. "Maybe if we tell someone, it could help. I can go with you."

I bit my lip, feeling nervous. "I don't know, Ben. I'm too scared. I don't think I can."

"That's okay, Ava. Maybe later then," Ben said, trying to cheer me up.

I looked at Ben. After sharing my worries with him, I felt a little better, but I was still scared. "What should I do? I feel stuck," I said.

"Talking might help," Ben said with a smile. "You don't need all the answers now. Let's focus on what could make you happier."

I nodded slowly. "Thanks, Ben. I'm just worried it won't get any better."

"It's okay to feel worried," Ben replied. "You're not alone. We'll work it out together."

I felt a little better, knowing I wasn't alone. But I was still scared of Emily and her friends. "I can write down what I want to say, even if I never share it."

"That's a great idea," Ben nodded. "Writing it down can help you see it better. You don't have to decide right away what to do with it. You know?"

I thought about this, feeling the warm sun on my face. "Yeah, I know," I said, feeling a bit braver. "Thanks for listening."

"Anytime, Ava. Remember, you're braver than you feel right now," Ben said, patting my shoulder.

We sat together a bit longer, hearing the distant sounds of laughter as I started to feel a tiny bit braver deep down inside.

Finding the Magic Pen

After I chatted with Ben, I felt that little spark of bravery light up inside me. I took a detour through the park on my way home. There, I stumbled upon a shiny, golden pen on the leaves. It looked magical, so I couldn't help but scoop it up.

At home, in my cozy little room, I sat down at my desk by the window, the afternoon light spilling across my notebook. I whispered to myself, "Let's see if you write as pretty as you look."

To my astonishment, the pen vibrated gently in my hand, and a warm, friendly voice emerged. "Hello, Ava! Ready to create some magic together?"

I almost dropped it. "What? A pen can talk?" I asked, my eyes wide.

Yes, I can!" the pen said with a giggle. "I'm here to help you find your voice and speak up!"

"Oh my goodness, You—you can talk, and I can understand you," I gasped, hardly believing what was happening.

Feeling a mix of excitement and curiosity, I paused for a moment. Then, I asked, "Can you help me say things without being scared?"

"That's exactly why I'm here," the pen buzzed. "Let's start by writing something. What's been on your mind?"

I thought about everything — the playground, Ben's encouragement, and how I wished I could speak up.

"What about how I can stand up to the mean girls at school?" I asked, thinking of Emily and her friends, who often made fun of me.

"Perfect," the pen buzzed. "Imagine what you'd want to say to them."

So, I wrote a dialogue, practicing the words I'd never dared to say out loud. "Why do you guys tease me? What did I ever do to you?"

I wrote, my hand guided by the pen's gentle vibration. "I wish we could be friends, or at least not enemies."

"Great job, you can try that. Keep me in your pocket."

The next day, with the pen tucked securely in my pocket, I felt ready.

At recess, when Emily and her friends started whispering and giggling as they looked my way, something inside me snapped. I walked straight up to them, my heart pounding. "You can do this, Ava. Just like we practiced," I told myself.

"Emily, can I talk to you?" My voice shook a little, but the pen pressed against my side seemed to steady me.

Emily raised an eyebrow, looking surprised. "What do you want, Ava?"

I took a deep breath, remembering the lines I'd written.

"Why do you guys always tease me?" I asked, the words tumbling out. "What did I do to you?" I managed to say, trying to sound stronger than I felt.

Her friends quieted, watching us.

Emily hesitated, then shrugged. "I don't know. It's just what we do, I guess."

I frowned, my fear mingling with frustration. "But just because it's what you do, doesn't make it right. It hurts me," I admitted, feeling the pen's warmth encourage me to keep going. "If we could all get along, that would be nice. Or at least not upset each other?"

Emily bit her lip, glancing at her friends, who were watching closely. "I... I guess you're right. We didn't think it was such a big deal."

"But it is to me," I said, finding strength in my honesty.

Emily looked at her friends, then back at me. She seemed unsure, then finally nodded. "Okay, we'll stop."

As I walked away, my legs felt like jelly, but I was proud. I had done it! I had stood up for myself with the words I had practiced, and it worked.

Ben was waiting for me by the swings. "I saw that, Ava! You were awesome!"

"I was terrified, Ben, but somehow, saying those words out loud... it made me feel powerful." And I told him about the magic pen.

"That's great, but I think you have the courage inside you. The pen just helped a little," Ben said with a grin.

That evening, as I wrote in my notebook, I didn't write a fairy tale or an adventure. Instead, I wrote about my day, facing Emily and her friends, and how I felt afterward. The pen hummed softly as if it were proud of me.

"Dinner's ready!" Mom called from downstairs.

I tucked the pen into my notebook and headed down, ready to share my victory at the table. My family would be so excited to hear how I stood up to the bullies. And I couldn't wait to tell them—especially since I knew the real challenge was still ahead.

The Magic Pen is Lost

After dinner that night, I told my family about my big win. They were all super duper proud of me, and I felt like a shiny star! But guess what? My shiny star day was about to face a huge challenge!

The next morning, I clutched my magical pen tightly as I headed to school. I was buzzing with excitement, ready to share my new confidence with everyone.

In the library, I was surrounded by books about knights, pirates, and all sorts of heroes. I was so caught up in choosing the perfect adventure book. I didn't notice the pen slipping from my pocket.

Later, in the classroom, I reached for the pen and realized—it was gone!

"Ben!" I whispered frantically, "My pen! It's missing!"

"I feel like I left it in the library," I told him, my eyes wide with worry.

Ben tried to reassure me. "We'll look again after class. It's got to be there somewhere."

As the clock ticked slowly, I felt more and more desperate. Finally, the bell rang, and I bolted out of my seat, nearly knocking over my chair.

Ben caught up with me.

"Slow down, Ava! Running won't make the pen appear!"

But I was already halfway to the library, my heart racing. We scoured the place again, looking behind every book and under every shelf. The librarian, Mrs. Finch, noticed our frantic search.

"What are you two looking for so eagerly?" she asked, her glasses sliding down her nose.

"It's my pen, Mrs. Finch! My magical talking pen!" I blurted out, my voice trembling. "It's gone, and I feel like I've lost my voice along with it."

Mrs. Finch looked puzzled but smiling. "A talking pen, you say? I don't know about talking but it must be a special pen. Let's have one more look around, shall we?"

We searched for another tense, but no luck. The pen was truly gone. I slumped against a bookshelf, feeling defeated.

I felt a lump in my throat as I walked back to class. The empty pocket of my jacket felt heavy. Without the pen, I suddenly felt all my new confidence draining away. How was I supposed to speak up now?

The rest of the day was really hard. In class, the teacher asked a question. I knew the answer but couldn't find the courage to raise my hand. The words stuck in my throat.

During lunch, Emily and her friends whispered. They did it again. This time, I was too scared to face them. I remembered Ben's words about magic being within me. It was hard to believe, especially without it in my hand.

At recess, Ben noticed I was upset. "What's wrong, Ava?" he asked.

I sighed, "I don't know if I can be brave without it."

Ben looked concerned. "But Ava, you were brave before. Remember? You stood up to Emily. The pen helped, but those words came from you."

I nodded, but I wasn't sure. It felt like the pen had given me superpowers, and now they were gone.

Discovering Inner Strength

After school, I went home. I sat in my room, looking at my empty notebook. I tried to write, but without the pen, my ideas felt stuck. I missed its cheerful buzz and the way it made everything easier.

Mom noticed me moping around after dinner. She sat down next to me on the couch with a worried look. "Ava, what's on your mind? You seem quiet today."

I hugged a cushion tight to my chest. "Mom, I lost my magic pen... the one that helps me talk. Now, everything feels so hard."

Mom wrapped her arm around me. "Oh, sweetheart, I know that pen was special, but I believe in you. You've got your magic inside, you know." Her voice was full of hope and encouragement.

The next day, I had to give a presentation in class. I stood in front of everyone, my hands shaking. I started to speak, but my voice was so quiet that someone in the back said, "Speak up. We can't hear you."

I wanted to crawl into a hole and hide. I missed my pen so much.

During recess, I found Ben standing by the sandbox. I walked over to him, and we started talking.

"Ben, it was awful," I blurted out. "I tried to give my presentation, and my voice just... disappeared. Someone even told me to speak up because they couldn't hear me."

Ben looked at me seriously. "That sounds tough. But you know, everyone has those moments. Maybe you just need a bit of practice without the pen."

"I guess," I sighed. "But how do I practice being brave?"

"Let's start small," Ben suggested. "What if you just try saying 'hello' to one person you usually don't talk to? Just being you."

I nodded slowly, feeling a tiny spark of hope. "Okay, I can try that. Thanks, Ben."

The following day, I challenged myself to say "hello" to someone new at school. I chose Mika, a girl I'd never spoken to from my math class. My heart raced as I walked up to her.

"Hi, Mika!" I managed to say, my voice a little shaky.

She looked up, surprised, then smiled. "Hey, Ava! What's up?"

"Nothing much. I just wanted to say hi," I replied, feeling a thrill of accomplishment as she smiled back.

"That's cool, Ava. See you in class!" Mika waved as she walked away, and confidence swelled inside me.

I couldn't wait to share my small victory at dinner that night. "Mom, Dad, I talked to someone new today!"

"That's wonderful, Ava!" Mom said, her eyes lighting up. "You're stepping out of your comfort zone."

Dad grinned at me across the table. "See? You're stronger than you thought. Keep it up, kiddo."

Their encouragement made me feel even more determined. Each day, I set a new, small challenge for myself, like joining a conversation at lunch or volunteering to answer a question in class. My confidence grew with each step.

One evening, I was writing in my journal about my day's brave moments. Mom popped her head into my room. "Writing again?" she asked with a smile.

"Yeah, I'm writing about something brave I did today," I said, showing her my journal filled with entries.

Mom sat beside me, reading over my shoulder. "These are fantastic, Ava! You're not just finding your voice; you're sharing it too."

I smiled really big, feeling super proud of myself.

A few days later, during recess, I saw Emily looking sad and alone. I remembered how talking had helped me. I wondered if I could help her. So, I decided to walk over to her. "Hey, Emily, everything okay?"

She looked up, a bit startled. "Oh, it's just a rough day. Thanks for asking, Ava."

We talked briefly, and by the end of recess, Emily was smiling. "Thanks for listening. I didn't think you would."

As I walked away, I realized how good it felt to make a difference with just a few kind words.

I told Ben about my conversation with Emily during our usual meeting under the tree after school. He gave me a high five. "You're amazing! Who would've thought? You are helping Emily—that's the real magic."

I laughed, feeling proud and empowered. "It feels good to help. Maybe I don't need a magic pen after all."

Ben nodded. "Exactly! Your magic was never about the pen. It's in your words and courage."

At first, losing the magic pen felt like the end of the world. But with each new day, I was ready to face any challenge. Now, I knew I had real magic inside me.

Ava's Lesson:

Ava learned she did not need a magic pen to speak up bravely. She discovered that her real strength comes from within, supported by the encouragement of her friends and family. Through her experiences, she realized that every child has the potential to be brave and make a difference simply by using their voice.

Message to you from Ava:

"Speaking up is about sharing your thoughts and feelings. You don't need to be afraid to speak up about what matters to you; bravery comes from within, and your words can make an incredible difference in the world! Keep shining and sharing your thoughts." Love, Ava

CHAPTER 5

The Secret in the Grove

I was running as fast as my legs could carry me. I was racing away. Big, loud raindrops started to splash all around. The sky suddenly turned dark, and the wind whistled through the trees. I needed to find a dry spot fast!

"Come on, Sai, you can make it!" I told myself this as I spotted the old grove up ahead. It's my favorite secret spot near our village in Thailand.

Just as I dove under the thick leaves of a big tree for cover, I bumped right into something huge, solid, and unexpectedly... gray. I yelped and stumbled back, my heart skipping a beat.

"Whoa, sorry! I didn't see you there," I said, my eyes wide as I looked up in complete surprise.

The huge gray thing turned around. It was an elephant! Not just any elephant but a young one. He looked as surprised as I was. It was the first time I'd ever been this close to an elephant without any fences between us. He was young but still much taller than me, a gentle giant with kind eyes.

"Hi there, I'm Sai. What's your name?" I giggled, knowing he couldn't answer.

He flapped his big ears and made a soft noise. It sounded friendly.

"Are you hiding from the rain, too?" I pulled out a banana from my bag. "Want a snack while we wait for the storm to pass?"

He gently took the banana with his trunk, and I couldn't help but laugh.

"You must like bananas a lot! I think I found your name. I'll call you Suay, which means 'beautiful' in Thai," I said, deciding right there.

"Suay, is this your first time meeting a human?" I looked into his big, kind eyes, wondering if he was just as surprised as I was.

I guess I had never thought I'd meet an elephant up close like this. It was like finding a hidden treasure right here in our village.

"Suay, do you live here all by yourself?" I looked around, wondering if there were more elephants.

He munched on the banana, and I took that as a yes.

"We can be friends if you want. I don't have many friends, and you seem nice," I chatted, feeling braver with each word.

We stood there, me talking and Suay listening, until the rain stopped and the sun peeked through the clouds. I knew then that we were going to be great friends.

"Let's explore this place tomorrow, Suay! Maybe we'll find a secret or two," I whispered, feeling warm inside.

He lifted his trunk and made a happy sound. Tomorrow, it will be our first adventure together.

Unraveling the Mystery

As Suay and I walked through the grove, the morning sun peeked through the trees. I always knew where to find him. He was near the big, old banyan tree. That's where we first met during a sudden thunderstorm. Ever since that day, I offered him a banana. He shyly accepted. We have become inseparable friends.

Today, we were explorers on a big mission. I noticed odd marks on the trees. I also saw strange footprints on our last adventure.

"We've got to find out what these mean, Suay," I told him, feeling like a detective in one of my storybooks.

"See these scratches, Suay?"

I pointed at a tree as we walked.

"I think they're too high up for small animals. And look at these footprints; they're much bigger than mine!" I added, frowning a bit.

Suay made a low rumble, sniffing the ground and looking concerned. I patted his trunk.

"Don't worry, we'll figure this out together," I told him.

I was practicing positive self-talk. "We're smart, we're brave, and we can solve mysteries, right?"

Suay rumbled lowly, his trunk sniffing the ground anxiously. I gently patted his side to comfort him. "Suay, we've got this," I said out loud, building up our confidence.

"We're smart, we're brave, and we can solve mysteries, right?"

Just then, I remembered something important.

"You know, Suay, my grandma always used to say, 'Talk to yourself like you'd talk to a friend when things get tough.'" I smiled at the memory.

"So, whenever I feel scared or unsure, I remind myself of all the brave and smart things I can do. It really helps!" I told him, feeling the words lift my spirits like they always do.

As we followed the trail of clues, I kept talking with Suay.

"It's like a puzzle, isn't it? We have to find all the pieces."

Suddenly, Suay stopped and trumpeted softly. He pulled me back with his trunk just in time. Right in front of us, cleverly hidden a large net under a mess of leaves. I gasped; my eyes wide with shock.

"That's a trap, Suay!"

"Watch out!" I shouted, my voice shaking as much as my hands. It was so scary to think that someone had put something so dangerous right where we walked. My heart was beating so fast that it wanted to jump out of my chest and run away!

"Why would someone do this?" I muttered, feeling mad. Granddad had told me about traps like this, but seeing one for real made me furious.

Suay must have sensed the danger before I even noticed it, his quick action made us safe.

"You're amazing, Suay," I praised him, trying to catch my breath and slow my pounding heart.

"How did you spot that?" I asked, looking at him with wonder. Suay just nudged me gently as if reminding me to stay alert and careful.

I felt all jittery inside, but I remembered what I always told myself: "Confidence is like a muscle—the more you use it, the stronger it gets." Taking a deep breath, I looked around carefully.

"We need to make sure there aren't any more traps around," I decided.

Together, we marked the spot with a bright cloth. I had brought them. "This will alert other animals and friends to be careful," I told Suay.

Feeling like a hero in my adventure, we headed back to the village. It was time to tell everyone what we had found. I practiced what I'd say all the way home, trying to sound as brave and confident as I felt with Suay by my side.

As we walked, I turned to Suay and said, "You know, my grandparents are waiting at home. They used to take care of our village just like this when they were my age. Now they're older, and it's hard for them to handle these things, so it's up to us now, Suay." I puffed out my chest a little, feeling brave.

"We've got to keep everyone safe, just like they did."

When we reached the village, I gathered all the villagers at the old banyan tree. My stomach was doing somersaults, but I remembered my positive self-talk.

"You can do this, Sai. You're not alone; Suay is here."

I took a deep breath and started to share our discovery, feeling the weight of my grandparents' trust on my shoulders.

Standing in front of them, I slowly took a big breath. "Everyone, Suay and I found something important in the grove. There's a big trap hidden under the leaves. It could hurt any of us—our children, our animals. We need to do something about it."

The villagers murmured, looking worried but also a bit unsure. Mr. Niran, the oldest villager, stepped forward.

"Sai, are you sure? Who would do such a thing?"

"Yes, I'm sure," I replied, my voice steady.

"Suay and I saw it with our own eyes. We marked the spot. We can show you. We don't want anyone to get hurt."

Mrs. Lek, who always liked to organize things, nodded. "What do you think we should do, Sai?"

I felt my confidence surge. "We should have a village meeting. We can talk about how to keep our grove safe. Maybe even make some signs to warn people and patrol the area," I suggested.

"That's a very good idea, Sai," Mr. Niran said, smiling at me. "You're a brave girl to bring this to us."

Everyone agreed, and they started talking about what to do next.

As we walked home, Suay nudged me gently, and I knew he was proud of me too. "We did it, Suay!

We are helping to protect our home," I whispered, feeling my "confidence muscle" stronger than ever.

Rallying the Village

The next day, the villagers gathered around, the air buzzing with concern and curiosity. Everyone agreed something had to be done.

"We need to keep watch at night," I suggested, remembering the courage.

"Who will help keep our grove safe?"

Several hands shot up. The kids were eager to help with their parents and older siblings.

"I'll help with the night watches," offered Mr. Arun. He was a seasoned farmer who knew the land better than anyone.

"And I'll organize patrols," said Mrs. Chitra. She was quick-thinking and respected by everyone.

"I can bring snacks," added Ley. He always thinks about the next meal. This made everyone chuckle.

Villagers, young and old, prepared together. They were ready to protect our beloved grove.

That night, under the twinkling stars, we started our first watch. My stomach was a bundle of nerves.

"You can do this, Sai," I whispered to myself. "You're smart, you're brave, and you're not alone." Suay stood next to me, watching me with his kind eyes. "I need to protect him no matter what," I said to myself.

Several nights passed without incident. Then, we heard the unmistakable sound of twigs snapping.

"Stay calm," I said softly. My voice was barely a whisper. I peered into the darkness with our group. We all crouched low, watching. Two shadowy figures approached. They stepped carefully. But, they clearly aimed for where we found the trap.

"It's now or never," I thought, my "confidence muscle" tensing.

"Hey!" I yelled, stepping out of our hiding spot and beaming my flashlight.

"What are you doing here?" I demanded. My voice echoed in the quiet night, strong and clear.

"We... we were just walking," Mr. Somchai stuttered, but the tools in their hands told another story.

I stepped closer, anger flaring within me. "Walking? At night? With shovels?" I challenged, my voice sharp.

"We know about the traps," I said, my voice stronger than I felt. "You can't do this here. It's dangerous and wrong. It could have hurt someone or Suay!"

Mr. Somchai looked at his brother, then at all of us kids standing together, and finally at Suay.

"We didn't mean any harm," he mumbled.

"I... I'm sorry, Sai. We were trying to catch birds or something to sell... to make some money. Times are tough," he confessed, his voice cracking.

"There is no excuse for harming our forest or our friends!" I shot back, my words like arrows.

"This is our home! How would you feel if someone set a trap where your children play?"

"You're right, Sai. We didn't think it through. It was wrong, and we're sorry," he admitted, his head bowed.

"Okay, fine. We hear your apology," I said. I could feel every eye in the grove on me. It fueled my courage.

"But let's work together to make things right and make sure everyone feels safe again."

He nodded slowly. "We will help. We'll make it right, Sai. We promise."

After they left, everyone cheered. "You did it, Sai!" Pim hugged me. "You really stood up to them!"

The next day, the whole village gathered to discuss the future of our grove near the banyan tree. The air was filled with excitement. Suay stood beside me, his trunk swaying gently.

Mr. Arun is holding a worn hat in his hands. He was the first to speak.

"Sai, what you did last night showed us all something. It showed how important it is to protect our grove and the animals," he said. His voice was loud and clear for everyone to hear.

"Yes," added Mrs. Chitra, nodding strongly. "And we should all help! What if we start by building a safe place for all the wildlife, like a sanctuary?"

"I love it!" I said, excited. "We can set up signs and clear paths to keep our animals and children safe."

"Let's do it!" a chorus of voices replied.

Over the next few weeks, everyone pitched in. Men and women, old and young, everyone worked together. We built fences where needed. We also made signs that read: "Protected Wildlife Sanctuary."

The day we finished, Mr. Arun called everyone.

"Thanks to Sai and Suay, we've done something wonderful here," he announced, his face beaming with pride.

"I've never been prouder of our village," Mrs. Chitra added. "Look what we can achieve when we work together!"

Everyone cheered, clapping and looking around at the safe haven we had created together.

I tugged gently on Suay's trunk and whispered to him. "Look at everyone! We did something big, didn't we?"

Suay trumpeted softly, and I laughed, feeling happy and proud.

"I used to be the quiet girl who hardly spoke up," I said, speaking just to Suay as we watched the joy spread through our village. Helping save our grove made me feel so strong."

"And you know what?" I smiled at him.

"Just like our muscles get stronger when we use them, my confidence has grown with every challenge we face."

Suay nuzzled me gently, and I knew he understood. Everyone was still celebrating and I felt like I truly belonged.

Sai's Lesson:

Sai learned that even small actions can make a big difference. She discovered that facing challenges helps you grow stronger. By standing up for what she believed in, Sai found her strength and her courage.

Message to you from Sai:

"Every challenge is a new adventure, a chance to make your confidence muscle stronger! Remember, every time you try, you learn something new. Keep being curious and brave. You can do amazing things!" Love, Sai

CHAPTER 6

Can Honesty Solve the Mystery?

I dashed through the neighborhood Park. I heard a soft whimper. Behind a tree, a tiny, brown puppy looked at me. It had big, pleading eyes.

"Hey there, what are you doing all alone?" I asked, kneeling beside the puppy. It wagged its tail and stared at me. The puppy seemed lonely and in need.

I felt nervous about my parents. They've always said no to pets because of allergies and mess. Still, I couldn't leave the puppy alone. The thought of sneaking around made my cheeks warm. And I was excited about my secret plan, my hands trembling.

"What if I keep you hidden, just in the backyard? I could make a cozy spot for you behind the shed," Hannah said softly to herself, imagining the secret hideout.

"And I can bring you food when no one's watching. We could play there after school."

The puppy gave a small yelp as if agreeing with my plan. I smiled, feeling a mix of excitement and worry.

"Okay, just for now," I decided, gently scooping it into my arms.

"I'll take care of you. It'll be our little secret."

Holding the puppy close, I felt its heartbeat. I was happy but also a little worried. It seemed tough. But the way it looked at me, so thankful, made me think we could make it through.

I have a new friend. I really, really wanted to keep the puppy safe, no matter what.

Building the Bond

As the school bell rang, my friends gathered their things and turned to me.

"Hannah, do you want to come to the park with us?" Lena asked, bouncing on her toes.

I bit my lip, glancing at the clock.

"Um, I can't today," I said, feeling a tug in my heart. "I gotta get home—uh, I have a big project to work on!"

"Another project? You always have a project!" Max chimed in, looking puzzled.

I nodded quickly, swinging my backpack over my shoulder.

"Yeah, it's super important. Maybe next time!" I added, dashing out of the classroom before they could ask more questions.

After school, I found Buddy behind the shed.

"Hey, Buddy! Look!" I whispered, holding up a small bag of treats. His tail wagged, and he yapped, bouncing around me.

"Remember, be quiet," I said, laughing as he tried to catch the treats I threw.

"Sit, Buddy, sit!" I encouraged. He'd plop down, his eyes locked on the treat in my hand.

"Good boy!" I'd cheer, giving him a gentle pat.

One evening, I sighed as I sat with Buddy, stroking his soft fur.

"Buddy, what am I gonna do? I wish I could tell Mom and Dad about you," I murmured, watching his ears perk up as he listened.

"I just... I don't want them to say you have to go away. You're my best friend," I confessed, my voice shaky. Buddy nuzzled his nose against my cheek, and I felt tears prick my eyes.

"But it's so hard to keep you a secret." I feel all twisty inside.

"Do you think they'd understand if they knew how much I loved you?"

Buddy gave a soft bark, and I smiled, wiping away a tear.

"Maybe we can show them how good and quiet you are. Maybe then they'll let you stay."

I pondered, my heart torn between the truth and my fear of losing my furry friend.

"We'll figure it out, Buddy. Together," I whispered, feeling a bit braver with him.

The Mysterious Disappearance

I rushed home from school, eager to see Buddy, but as I got closer to my house, my steps slowed. The space behind the old shed was empty. "Buddy?" I called, my voice shaking. I hoped he would come out, but there was only silence.

Panic gripped me. I searched everywhere in the yard, checking behind bushes and the side of the shed, but there was no sign of Buddy. "He might be lost... or worse," I thought, tears welling up.

Then, a scary thought struck me: "What if Buddy has another family looking for him?"

Determined to find Buddy, I acted like a detective.

"I must do something," I said, clenching my fists. Then, I went from door to door, asking neighbors about a small brown dog. Some said, "Sorry, no honey," or "I'll keep an eye out, Hannah."

I recruited my friends the next day.

"Guys, we need to find Buddy. He's lost and might be scared!" I explained it at school. Lena, Max, and others nodded, ready to join the search.

"Let's be pet detectives!" Max declared, making us all giggle despite the worry.

Uncovering Clues

Our little detective group followed a trail of paw prints to Mrs. Jenkins' backyard.

"Look! The prints go right up to her flower beds," Lena pointed out. We started digging carefully, hoping to find a clue.

Just then, whoosh! The air filled with water as sprinklers burst to life.

"Aaah!" we all screamed, jumping back, but it was too late. We were soaked, our clothes sticking to us, dripping wet. We looked at each other and burst into laughter, the tension of our search turning into a wet, giggly mess.

As we stood there, dripping and laughing, I thought about all the secrets I'd been keeping.

"Maybe I should've told my parents about Buddy from the start," I mumbled to Lena, who was wringing out her shirt.

"Yeah, secrets can be tough," she agreed, giving me a soggy hug.

"But hey, now we have a funny story to tell!" Max chimed in, trying to make me feel better.

Mrs. Jenkins came out then, chuckling at our drenched detective crew.

"Oh, you kids! Always up to something," she laughed, handing us towels. "What brought you into my sprinkler trap?"

"We were looking for clues... for my lost puppy, Buddy," I confessed, my voice quiet. "I kept him a secret, and now he's gone."

Mrs. Jenkins nodded, her smile kind.

"Secrets are heavy to carry, my dear. It's always best to share your worries and joys. It makes them easier to handle, you know?"

I nodded, understanding her words.

"I guess I need to start being honest, even if it's scary," I thought, feeling braver.

"Exactly, Hannah," Mrs. Jenkins said. "Being honest is important, especially with those who care about you."

Armed with towels and new resolve, I knew what to do next. I had to be honest with my parents. But first, I needed to find Buddy, with a little help from my friends.

After the sprinkler surprise at Mrs. Jenkins' house, we gathered around the edge of her garden, dripping and plotting our next move. Suddenly, Buddy's disappearance hit me hard.

"Where else could he be?" Max asked, shaking water out of his hair.

"I don't know, but we've got to keep looking,"
I replied, trying to sound braver than I felt. "He
couldn't have gone far, right?"

"Let's split up," Lena suggested.

"That way, we can look everywhere faster.
Hannah, can you go look in the park again? Max
and I will go check the streets over there."

I nodded and started back towards the park, my
favorite place with Buddy.

"Buddy!" I called out as I walked, hoping for any
sign of him. My voice echoed back, empty and
alone.

"Where are you, Buddy?" I whispered, feeling
the weight of the secret I had kept. If I had just
told my parents about him, maybe he wouldn't be
lost now. Maybe we'd be playing in our backyard
instead of me searching every shadow and bush.

As the sun began to set, the air grew cooler,
and my hope started to fade. I met up with Lena
and Max again, who both shook their heads; they
hadn't found Buddy either.

"We're not giving up, are we?" Max looked at me,
his face serious.

"No," I said, my voice firm despite my trembling lip. "We can't. Buddy needs us."

"What about tomorrow?" Lena suggested. "We can make some 'Lost Puppy' posters and put them up around the neighborhood."

"Yeah, that's a great idea!" I felt a small spark of hope.

"And maybe I should finally talk to my parents. Tell them everything. They might help us, too."

"You really think so?" Max asked, his brow furrowed.

"I don't know, but I shouldn't keep this a secret any longer. It's not right, and I feel heavy," I admitted. "But I'm not sure when to tell them."

The Hidden Surprises

The next day, we explored the unfamiliar part of the neighborhood. We followed the mysterious paw prints.

"Where do you think these go?" Max asked, pointing at the prints that disappeared into a small, wooded area.

"Let's find out," I said, my heart pounding with a mix of nervousness and worries.

As we pushed through the brush, we saw a cozy house. It had a big, fenced yard filled with dogs of all sizes. They were playing and barking happily.

"Wow, look at all these dogs!" Lena exclaimed.

Just then, a woman with kind eyes and a bright smile came out to greet us.

"Hello there! I'm Jennifer. How can I help you kids?"

"We're looking for a lost puppy," I started, but a slight pause.

"He's small, brown, big eyes... I've been taking care of him, but he got lost."

Jennifer nodded, her eyes softening. "You must be worried. Come on in, and let's see if we can find your friend."

Inside, Jennifer led us to a small room where newly rescued dogs were kept. And there, in a cozy corner, was Buddy! His tail wagged furiously when he saw me.

"Buddy!" I cried out, rushing to the fence. Tears blurred my vision as I reached through to pet him.

"I've missed you so much!"

He licked my fingers, yipping happily.

"Looks like he missed you too," Jennifer observed with a chuckle.

Max patted my back. "He looks good, Hannah. You did the right thing looking for him."

"Can he come home with me now?" I asked Jennifer, wiping a tear from my cheek.

She knelt beside me, her expression serious but kind.

"Let's make sure it's okay with your parents first. It's important they know and agree to him coming home."

I swallowed hard, knowing she was right.

"I'm going to tell them everything tonight. Could you please keep Buddy safe until I can come back?" I asked.

"Of course, he'll be here waiting for you," Jennifer assured me, giving my shoulder a gentle squeeze.

"I promise I'll be back soon, Buddy," I said, giving his ear a soft tug. He nuzzled my hand, his little eyes trusting.

On the way back, my nerves were on edge, but I also felt relieved.

"I'll tell them about finding Buddy and how I've cared for him," I said to Lena and Max.

"That's really brave of you, Hannah," Max said, looking impressed.

"And we'll help you," Lena said quickly. "We'll tell them how well you've cared for him. They must understand."

"Thanks, you guys. I think it's going to be okay," I replied, feeling stronger with my friends by my side.

Honesty and A New Beginning

That evening, as the last rays of the sun turned the sky pink and orange, I sat on the living room carpet, twisting my fingers together nervously. Mom and Dad sat on the couch, looking at me with curious eyes.

"Mom, Dad, I have something really, really important to tell you," I started, my heart thumping loudly in my chest.

"What is it, sweetheart?" Mom asked, her voice gentle, making it a tiny bit easier to speak.

I took a deep breath and let it all out.

"I found a puppy in the park a few weeks ago. He was all alone and really scared. I... I didn't tell you because I thought you'd make me give him back. So, I hid him in our backyard. I named him Buddy." I rushed the words out, hoping they'd understand.

My parents listened, their expressions softening with each word. When I finished, there was a brief silence—a moment that felt like it stretched forever.

Dad raised his eyebrows. "You've been hiding a puppy?"

I nodded, feeling my cheeks warm.

"Yes, but he got lost, and then my friends helped me find him at Jennifer's house. She rescues dogs."

Mom's expression softened. "Oh, Hannah."

Dad leaned forward; his eyebrows raised a little.

"You've been taking care of a puppy all by yourself?"

"I'm really sorry I didn't tell you," I confessed, looking down at my fidgeting hands.

Mom exchanged a look with Dad, then both of them turned back to me.

"Hannah, we're proud of you for helping Buddy when he was in trouble," Mom said, smiling softly.

"But you should have told us, honey," Dad added. "We could have helped you. It's important to be honest, even if you think we might say no."

"I'm sorry, I just didn't want to lose him. So, can I keep Buddy? Please?" I looked up hopefully.

Dad exchanged a look with Mom.

"Let's go meet Buddy this weekend," he said. "And we'll talk about it."

I jumped up, giving them both the biggest hug.

That weekend, we all went to Jennifer's rescue. Buddy zoomed over to me super fast as soon as he saw me, his tail wagging like crazy.

"This is Buddy!" I introduced him with a big smile.

"Buddy, this is my mom and dad!"

"He's very sweet," Mom said, giving Buddy a gentle pat. He nuzzled her hand, and I could tell she was falling in love with him just like I had.

Jennifer came over, smiling.

"I'm glad you brought your parents, Hannah. It's important to make sure everyone is on board."

"We've talked it over," Dad said, "and we'd like to adopt Buddy if that's all right."

"It's more than all right," Jennifer replied. "I think it's wonderful."

As we filled out the adoption papers, I felt like my heart would burst with happiness. I had Buddy, my parents were proud of me, and I'd learned a huge lesson about honesty.

"Buddy's going to be part of our family now," I said as we walked home, Buddy trotting happily beside us.

"Yes, he is," Mom confirmed, "And Hannah, we're proud of how you handled this. Remember, being honest helps solve more problems than it creates."

I nodded, squeezing Buddy's leash a little tighter in my hand.

"I won't forget," I promised. We laughed and chatted as we walked home together. We were ready to start this new chapter as a family. Honesty and lots of puppy cuddles would lead the way.

Hanna's lesson:

Hannah found out that telling the truth is very important because it helps solve problems and makes everyone happier, showing that honesty builds trust. She also learned that asking for help from grown-ups can make things easier and more fun.

Message to you from Hanna:

"Always remember, telling the truth and asking for help can make everything better and more fun!" Love, Hanna

CHAPTER 7

A Journey of New Beginnings

"Dinner time, Nova!" Mom called. Nova, queen of her cozy blanket fort, wasn't ready to leave, but she walked out and went inside the house. A big surprise was about to change everything.

The Unwanted News

After dinner, I ran back outside to my fort. I was adding a new block tower when Mom peeked through the blanket door.

"Nova, honey, come inside. We need to talk about something important," she said, her tone more concerned than usual.

Inside, Dad and Mom were sitting on the couch, looking kind of serious. I sat down on the corner of the couch, curious about what was going on.

"Nova," Dad began, "I got a big job offer today."

"A job? That's great, Daddy!" I clapped, thinking maybe I could get a new set of blocks.

"But, sweetheart, this job is in Japan," Dad said softly.

"Japan? Where's that?" I tried to remember my map puzzle.

"It's a country on the other side of the world. It's very different from here," Mom explained.

"And we've decided that we're going to move there," Dad added gently.

"Move to Japan?" I blinked, surprised.

"Yes, honey. It's a big decision, but we think it will be good for all of us," Mom said, giving me a reassuring look.

I thought about our little street, bike rides, and the park where I played with my friends. We had so much fun at the playground, and sometimes, Dad would take me for ice cream near the library. I couldn't imagine leaving all that.

"But what about my friends? What about my fort?" I felt tight in my throat as I spoke.

"You can build a new fort, and you'll make new friends," Mom said, trying to smile.

"But I like my friends here. I don't want new ones," I said, feeling stubborn.

"And what about my school? And Mrs. Brown? She is the best teacher ever. She said I'm almost ready to move to the big reading group!" I added, folding my arms.

Mom and Dad looked at each other, then back at me.

"We know it's hard, Nova. We're going to miss lots of things too. But sometimes, change can be an adventure," Dad said playfully, patting my back.

I wasn't sure about that. My adventures were supposed to be in the backyard or with my friends at the park—not far away where I couldn't see

Grandma on weekends or go to my favorite ice cream shop. I felt all mixed up inside.

"I don't want to go," I screamed, hoping to change their mind.

"We don't have to decide anything tonight," Mom said, pulling me into her lap. "Let's just think about it together, okay?"

I nodded, but inside, I really wished everything could just stay the same. Snuggled in Mom's hug, I wished I could hide in my fort where everything was safe and nothing ever changed.

The Journey Begins

The big moving day came way too fast. Boxes filled every corner of my room, and my heart felt super heavy. The goodbye party at the park was a blur of tears and hugs.

"Promise you'll write to me?" I asked Ellie, trying not to let my voice wobble.

"Every week! And don't forget, we can video chat!" Ellie squeezed my hand, her eyes shiny with tears.

Saying goodbye to Grandma was the hardest. Her hugs felt like warm blankets.

"You be brave, my little explorer," she whispered, her voice cracking a bit.

"Yeah, but I wish I didn't have to be," I mumbled, sniffling.

When we landed in Japan, everything felt different. Even our new house had rules like taking off shoes before coming in. I didn't like it.

"Why do we have to take off our shoes?" I complained as we stepped inside.

"It's respectful in Japan," Dad explained, lining up his shoes neatly.

"Seriously, we have to do that every time?" I asked, sounding annoyed.

"But I don't like it. It feels weird," I grumbled, kicking my shoes off into the corner.

The school was even more challenging. Everyone bowed to the teachers instead of waving hello, and I couldn't understand anyone.

"Why do we have to bow so much here?" I whispered to Mom after my first day, frustrated and near tears.

"It's polite here, like saying 'hello' in our way," Mom tried to explain as she unpacked another box.

Mom noticed I was still upset.

"In Japan, bowing is a way to show respect and kindness, just like when we say 'please' and 'thank you' at home. It's a big part of how they greet each other and show they care," she said gently.

"But it feels so strange. Why can't things be normal?" I frowned, sitting down hard on the floor.

"Things are normal for here, but Japan has a different culture. Did you know there are many different cultures in the world? America is just one of them. When someone comes to America, they think we are weird too." Mom giggled, sitting beside me and pulling me into a hug. "You'll get used to it, I promise."

"I don't think I ever will," I muttered, my arms crossed. I missed everything about home—my friends, school, and even just being able to say 'hi' without bowing. Japan felt like another planet, and I wasn't sure I wanted to live on it.

Unexpected Discoveries

Every day, I sat by myself during lunch because I couldn't speak Japanese well, and it seemed like everyone else already had their friends. The classroom buzzed with chatter I couldn't understand, and I felt like I was on an island all by myself.

A few weeks passed, and I was still not super happy about everything in Japan, but then something unexpected happened that made me start seeing things a little differently.

One day, during lunch, I was sitting alone again, poking at my food, when a teacher noticed me.

"Nova, why are you sitting all by yourself?" she asked, her English slow but clear.

"I don't have any friends yet," I admitted. It felt heavy in my heart.

"It's tough in the beginning, but you'll find a friend. You are kind and smart," she encouraged me, but I wasn't so sure.

After lunch, we had a special "Culture Day," and it all happened in the school's gym. It was full of stations for origami and calligraphy, and there was even a place to try on traditional Japanese clothes.

As I folded my paper crane, I was lost in thought about how much I missed home.

That's when Sakura bumped into me.

Her friendly smile and easy English were like a beam of sunlight on a cloudy day.

"Oops, sorry!" Sakura said as my paper slipped from my hands.

"Are you trying origami?" She picked up my paper and smiled at me.

"Yeah, it's harder than it looks, but really fun!" I replied, feeling a little spark of happiness.

"By the way, my name is Sakura. It means cherry blossom," she said with a smile.

"Oh, I'm Nova," I replied, feeling so happy that I could finally talk to someone.

"I used to make these all the time when I lived in the U.S.," Sakura mentioned casually.

"You lived in the U.S.? That's cool! No wonder your English is so good!" I exclaimed, feeling a bit relieved knowing she understood me so well.

"Yeah, for a few years. My English isn't perfect, but I can help if you need anything," she offered kindly.

"That would be amazing, thanks! My Japanese is pretty bad," I admitted with a laugh.

"Don't worry. Our teacher speaks a little English, but between us, we'll get you speaking Japanese in no time!" Sakura grinned, leading me to the ramen station.

"We also have sushi today," Sakura added, pointing to the food table.

I made a funny face. "I tried sushi once. It was... umm... not really my thing."

She laughed, and it wasn't a mean laugh. "Maybe you'll like ramen better. It's delicious!"

"Ramen? What's that?" I asked, curious.

"It's noodle soup. Very yummy! Let's try some!" Sakura suggested, and we went to get some ramen together.

It was delicious! Way better than the sushi I had tried. "This is really good!" I said, slurping the noodles.

"I'm glad you like it!" she smiled.

As we walked around the different stations, I couldn't help but wonder why Sakura lives in Japan now. "So, why did you move back to Japan?" I asked curiously.

"My dad's job brought us back. Sometimes, I miss the U.S., but I still keep in touch with a few friends. And I've made wonderful friends here, too," Sakura explained, handing me another bowl of steaming ramen.

Trying the ramen, I realized how nice it was to have someone who understood both where I came from and where I was now.

"This is so delicious, too!" I said, surprised by how much I liked it.

"I told you! Food is the best part of Culture Day," Sakura laughed.

"You know, I think Japanese food is the best in the world," she said with a proud smile.

"Why do you think it's the best?" I asked curiously.

"Because Japanese people care about what they eat. We take pride in our food—its preparation, ingredients, and even how it's served," Sakura explained, her eyes lighting up. "It's not just food; it's part of our culture, a way to show respect and care."

Tasting the ramen, I could see what she meant. It was delicious, and the way it was prepared and presented felt special.

"Yeah, I can see that!" I admitted, surprised by how much the flavors popped. When we were walking back to class, I had to ask Sakra about something I had noticed recently.

"Sakura, why is everything so clean here?" I asked.

I couldn't help but see how clean everything was. No trash on the streets, and no one ate while they walked. It was different.

"People here respect not only each other but also the places we live and visit," Sakura explained.

"We take care of our town like our home."

That made a lot of sense, and I started to see why things were the way they were here. Maybe Japan wasn't so bad after all. And with a friend like Sakura, I was beginning to feel like maybe I could fit in here, maybe I could even like it.

Overcoming and Embracing Change

With Sakura's help, I began to find my place in Japan. The school felt less lonely, and I learned more Japanese words every day. I started feeling like I belonged.

One day, during lunchtime at school, Sakura noticed that I was holding chopsticks awkwardly.

"Like this, Nova!" She gently adjusted my fingers. "You'll get it, don't give up!"

Suddenly, I didn't just pick up the rice ball but also a whole new confidence.

"I did it!" I exclaimed, proud of my small victory.

"See? You're becoming more Japanese every day!" Sakura giggled.

"And I learned to say 'Ohayou'—it sounds like 'Ohio,' where my cousin lives!" The joke made Sakura laugh even more.

"And don't forget 'Arigato'—like an alligator saying thank you!" I added, which made us both crack up.

One afternoon, Sakura and I were walking home from school when she asked, "Nova, do you want to come to karaoke (Karry-Oh-Key) with me and some friends this weekend?"

"Karaoke? What's that?" I asked, puzzled but curious.

"It's like a singing game where you can be a star! It's super fun, and it was invented in Japan!" Sakura explained, her eyes sparkling with excitement.

"Wow, really? I didn't know that!" I exclaimed in amazement. "And I'm not sure about singing... but it sounds like a lot of fun!"

I couldn't believe all the cool stuff that came from Japan—like anime, which I watched every Saturday morning. Sakura taught me Kendama, a game that was way harder than it looked.

"Next, I'll show you Mt. Fuji. It's beautiful! We can go when your friends from America visit?" Sakura suggested.

"That would be awesome! I can't wait to show them how much I've learned here," I said, excited about playing tour guide.

"Sakura, do you remember how scared I was when I first came here?" I asked.

"Yes, but look at you now. You're not just surviving; you're doing great!" Sakura cheered, sounding so proud.

That evening, surrounded by origami cranes in the dining room, I thought about my journey.

"Mom, Dad, I think I like it here," I said at dinner, surprising even myself a little.

"We knew you could do it, Nova," Mom said, smiling as she skillfully picked up a piece of sushi with her chopsticks.

"Yeah, I'm getting better with chopsticks, too," I said. Then, I picked up a piece of my favorite, shrimp tempura. It had a perfect, light, crispy outside.

"I love this. I could eat it every day!"

Mom chuckled, "It's delicious, but we can't have fried food every day."

"But sushi and I are still not best friends yet!"

As we all laughed together at dinner, I felt warm and happy inside. Going through so many changes and finally feeling at home here showed me how brave and strong I had become. Living in Japan turned into an amazing adventure, not just something I had to get used to.

Nova's lesson

Nova learned that change isn't just something to get through; it's a chance to have fun and discover new things. By trying new customs like taking off shoes indoors, she made new friends and found exciting places to play. She realized that every new challenge was an opportunity to grow and find joy.

Message to you from Nova:

"Always keep an open heart and mind because the most wonderful surprises often come from the least expected places."   *Love, Nova.*

CHAPTER 8

Inspiring Kind Hearts

In a small village in Africa, Zara looked up at the night sky with wonder.

Far away in the USA, Chloe did the same. Even though they were far apart, something magical was about to bring them together.

Zara and Chloe

"Class, today we're starting something quite special," my teacher announces as she gathers us around. "We're going to have pen pals from America!"

"What's a pen pal?" I ask, curious about the new word.

"A pen pal is a friend you make by sending letters across the world," she explains, her eyes twinkling.

"It's a wonderful way to learn about different places and people."

I am excited about writing to someone far away.

After school, I sit outside on a woven mat under the shade of a mango tree. The air is warm, and the sky fills with colors as the sun sets. I take a piece of paper, feeling the rough texture under my fingers. I think about the distance the letter will travel and the eyes that will read my words.

"Hello,

My name is Zara, and I'm eight years old. I live in a small village in Rwanda where not many people send letters anymore. It's hard to find stamps, and the nearest post office is far from our village, but I'm excited to write to you! I love to draw, especially the skies at dusk. They're full of color and wonder. Do you like to draw? On weekends, I help my mom at the busy market. It's full of noises, colors, and smells. What do you do for fun?

Warm wishes, Zara"

I imagine my letter sorting over lands and seas, carrying my words to someone new, someone who might soon become a friend.

Chloe in the US
Our classroom in Boston, MA, is full of chatter as our teacher announces our new project.

"Today, we're going to have pen pals from Rwanda in Africa!" she tells us, pointing to the country on a large map at the front of the room.

"You'll get to write letters and make a new friend from across the world!"

Not many people in Boston write letters these days. The idea of writing an actual letter feels special, almost like a secret adventure.

Back home, I sit at my desk, where my telescope is set up, pointing out the window. It's a clear night, and the stars are just beginning to appear. I pulled out a paper and started writing, thinking about what life might be like in Rwanda.

Hi!

My name is Chloe, and I'm eight years old. I live in Boston, where we rarely send letters anymore. We all use emails and messages because they're quicker, but I'm super excited to write to you! I love looking at the stars and learning about space. My telescope is one of my favorite things. What's your favorite subject in school? I also play soccer with my friends. Do you have a favorite sport or game?

I'm looking forward to learning about you, Chloe"

I seal the letter with a sticker of the Earth, feeling a connection to someone far away and imagining them under the same vast sky. I hope they write back soon. I'm eager to learn about their life and share more of mine.

Zara in Rwanda

After receiving the first letter, I thought a lot about my new friend, Chloe. Meanwhile, life in my village is tough these days. Dad says the crops didn't do well this season, which means less money to buy things we need. Sometimes, I wish I could help more.

"Zara, come help me sort these beans," Mom calls. I sit down beside her and sigh.

"Mom, will things get better?" I ask, picking up a handful of beans.

"We hope so, my dear. We just have to keep working hard," Mom replies with a tired smile.

At night, in our dimly lit tiny house, I write to Chloe. My hands ache, and my eyes droop, but sharing gives me hope. Our world is a mix of challenges and small beauties.

"Dear Chloe,

Life here is sometimes hard, but there are good parts, too! Every morning, my brother, sister, and I walk a long way to get water. It's really far, but I see the sun wake up the sky with big, bright colors. It's so pretty! My little brother asks, 'Why is the stream so far?' I tell him it's our adventure, and it makes him smile.

We don't have a lot of food, and sometimes I wish we had more, but my mom helps us feel okay about it. We laugh and tell stories, and that makes dinner feel special, even when there's not much to eat.

I dream about being a scientist one day. I want to learn about stars and find ways to help our plants grow better. My family cheers me on; they believe I can do it, and that makes me feel strong. How do you stay happy when things aren't easy?

Big hugs, Zara"

Chloe in the US

At home, the quietness sometimes feels overwhelming. I'm an only child, and with Mom and Dad always working, the house feels empty, almost echoing. School is busy, and I love learning, but it's lonely sometimes. Today, I tried to cook dinner by myself. It was just pasta, but at least it's something I can do on my own.

"Mom, look! I made dinner!" I call out proudly when she finally walks through the door.

"That's great, Chloe! I'm sorry I'm late again," she says, but her eyes are glued to her phone, and soon she's lost in emails.

Sighing, I went to my room and looked at the city lights. They didn't comfort me like the stars did. I turned to the paper on my desk and began writing to Zara.

"Dear Zara,

Thank you for your awesome letter! It sounds like you have cool adventures, even when you go get water. I love how you turn everything into a fun story!

Life here can be a bit lonely because I'm the only kid at home, and my mom and dad are always busy. But I try to make my own fun, like cooking! Today, I cooked spaghetti by myself. It turned out well. Sometimes, I imagined being a famous chef in a big restaurant, which made me laugh.

And guess what? When I feel lonely, I dance around my room or sing my favorite songs super loud. It makes me feel better and keeps me smiling.

What songs do you like to sing? Do you ever dance just for fun?

Your friend, Chloe"

Zara's Joyful Discovery

"Dear Chloe,

I was so happy to get your letter! It made me smile all day. I love how you turn cooking into a special activity. I don't cook much, but I do love to dance! Sometimes, after fetching water, my siblings and I dance under the open sky. It makes us forget we're tired.

Things have been really tough lately. It's hard when we don't have enough food, and seeing my parents worried makes me sad. I wish there were a way to make things better for my family.

What do you do when you wish you could help someone?

Your friend, Zara"

Chloe's Life-Changing Idea

After reading Zara's letter, Chloe felt a spark of inspiration. She knew she wanted to help Zara and her family and maybe even bring their community closer together.

"Dear Zara,

Your letter touched my heart. I've been thinking about how I could help. What if we started a project to raise money for your family? We could do something fun, like a star-themed charity event since we both love the stars so much! We could have games and sell things to raise money. Everyone could learn about the stars, too, and it would be a way to spread kindness. What do you think?

Your friend who wants to help, Chloe"

Planning the Starry Sky Project

Excited by Chloe's idea, Zara responded with enthusiasm.

"Dear Chloe,

I love your idea! It's amazing. A star-themed charity sounds magical. We could have a starry art contest or a bake sale with star-shaped cookies. What if we even had a storytelling night where we shared tales from around the world?

Let's make a plan. You could handle some things there, and I can do stuff here with my friends. We could both make posters and spread the word! I can't wait to hear what you think!

Your excited friend, Zara"

Chloe was overjoyed with Zara's response and quickly set to work.

Zara and Chloe started working on their project together. They shared lots of fun ideas. They built a special bridge of kindness and support across the world. Every letter they sent made them more excited and dedicated to their project. They wanted to make sure their starry sky project was a big success. It would be a shining light of hope and friendship.

Challenges and Surprises

Zara and Chloe began organizing their star-themed charity project. They quickly found that even the best plans can fail.

Determined not to let their friends down, Zara and Chloe brainstormed new ideas to keep their project moving forward.

Zara's Creative Solutions

"Dear Chloe,

I talked to my teacher, and she helped me come up with a plan. If it keeps raining, we can have the storytelling night at the school hall instead of outside. I also asked more friends to help with the posters, so I'm not doing it alone anymore. What do you think?

Your hopeful friend, Zara"

Chloe's Team Efforts

"Dear Zara,

Your ideas are great! I spoke to my parents, and they said we could have the bake sale at our community center. Also, I talked to the other kids at school about joining our project instead of having rival ones. They liked the idea of working together for a bigger cause. We're going to make this happen together!

Your excited friend, Chloe"

Zara's Starry Night at the School Hall

The school hall looked like a night sky full of stars. Lights twinkled everywhere, and paper stars hung from the ceiling. Everyone in the village came to see what was happening.

"Wow, Zara! It's like being outside at night but even more magical!" Beatrice said as she walked in, her eyes shining with excitement.

"It's beautiful!" another friend, Mwiza, shouted, twirling around under the paper stars.

I felt so happy seeing everyone's smiling faces.

"Welcome, everyone! Ready for a fun night of star stories?" I greeted the families coming through the door.

During the event, I got up to tell a story.

"Tonight, I'm going to tell you about Imigongo, special patterns from our place, Rwanda. They're made from cow dung and look a bit like the spirals in the stars," I explained. Everyone listened quietly, surprised to hear how our art connected to the stars.

After my story, one of the village elders, Mr. Kabera, came up to me.

"Zara, this is wonderful. We've never had something like this before. Thank you for bringing the stars to us," he said with a big smile.

My teacher, who helped us set up, was proud, too.

"You've done something special tonight. You've brought us all together beautifully," she told me, and I felt proud.

Everyone laughed, clapped, and enjoyed the stories. They also donated to help my family out.

It was amazing to see how happy and generous everyone was. It made me realize that we can do great things when we all come together.

Chloe's Bake Sale and Art Auction in Boston

The community center was filled with noise and fun as Chloe looked around at all the tables full of yummy treats and fantastic art pieces.

"Chloe, these star cookies taste like they're from space!" Emma giggled as she set up more Galaxy cupcakes.

"They're zooming off the table super fast!" Chloe laughed, handing a cookie to a little boy.

Over by the art, everyone was excited, watching and waiting to see who would win the paintings.

"Look at Mr. Thompson, go for that painting! He wants it, huh?" Mia pointed.

"He's after it like it's a piece of the moon!" Chloe chuckled, watching the fun bidding war.

The place was happy and loud. Friends helped by passing out cookies and cheering for the auction.

"Hey, Chloe, did you see how much your drawing made? You must be famous now!" Lucas joked, writing new numbers on the money board.

Chloe blushed and smiled.

"It's all because everyone here is so kind and helpful. We're all helping Zara and her family today. We're making a big difference!"

Everyone cheered even louder, happy to be part of something so special. The day was filled with laughs, tasty treats, and everyone helping. It was a perfect day. It showed how great things can be when everyone works together.

Zara and Chloe's Reflections and Dreams

The charity project with stars is all done.
Zara and Chloe were so amazed by what they accomplished. They couldn't believe how kind everyone was in their neighborhoods.

Zara in Rwanda

Chloe and her community helped; my family had enough extra money to buy food for our neighbors who needed help.

Mom and I packed boxes with food and blankets all afternoon. Walking down our street to deliver them, I felt we were on a special mission.

"Here you go, Mrs. Garcia," I said, handing over a heavy box.

"Thank you so much, Zara," she said, her voice warm and grateful.

"Mom, it's so wonderful to help everyone like this," I said as we walked to the next house.

"It sure is. You and Chloe have done more than just share things; you've spread a lot of joy here," Mom replied, squeezing my hand.

As we continued, I thought about Chloe and all her efforts.

"Mom, Chloe, and everyone far away cared so much. I'm going to remember this forever."

"That's the beauty of kindness, Zara. It connects people across the world."

I nodded, looking around at the happy faces.

"I hope we keep making a difference like this, Mom."

"We will, Zara. With friends like Chloe, the sky's the limit," she said, and we both laughed, feeling grateful and hopeful for the future.

Chloe in the US

A few weeks after their successful charity event, Chloe and her dad sat in the living room. They were reflecting on the great results of their work.

"Dad, do you remember how happy everyone was at the bake sale and auction?"

"I sure do. It was a special day. Everyone came together to help Zara and her family," her dad replied, his voice warm with pride.

"It feels amazing."

"I know, me too,"

"It's like magic! Giving is receiving. We get smiles and lots of happy feelings!"

"That's right, sweetheart. And those are the best gifts," her dad said, gently ruffling her hair.

Chloe felt inspired and grateful. The project had not only helped her make a difference, but it had also brought so much joy and new friends into her life.

Zara's Letter to Chloe

Dear Chloe,

Wow. Our project showed me the power of friendship and kindness. I've learned so much from working with you. Even though we are far apart, it feels like you are right here with me. Thank you for everything, Chloe.

We made such a great team, and I hope we will be friends forever. I promise to keep writing to you - my school, the stars, and my dreams. I want to hear all about your dreams, too!

One day, I want to learn about the stars. I also want to find new ways to help farmers in Rwanda grow more food. What big dreams do you have? Let's keep reaching for the stars together!

Big hugs, Zara

Chloe's Letter to Zara

Dear Zara,

You're right. Our project was more amazing than I thought! I'm so grateful for our friendship. It feels like we've built a bridge of kindness from here to Rwanda.

I promise to keep sending letters and sharing my adventures with you. You've inspired me a lot, and I can't wait to see the great things we'll do together and in our parts of the world.

I dream of exploring space. I also want to see how kids live and go to school in other countries. I could visit you in Rwanda one day!

Yes, let's always keep reaching for the stars and dreaming big dreams!

Forever friends, Chloe

Zara and Chloe's lesson

Zara and Chloe learned that being kind and working together can help anyone, no matter how far apart they are. They discovered that even little acts of kindness can make a big difference, making friends and their communities happier and closer.

Message to you from Zara:

"Always be kind. Every bit of kindness you share makes the world brighter!" Love, Zara

Message to you from Chloe:

"Hey girls, always believe in the power of friendship and dreaming big—it can take you amazing places!" Love, Chloe

CHAPTER 9

Diving into Dreams

A curious third grader named Jade loves to swim, but she is nervous about racing. She finds an amazing book in her school library—could it change everything for her?

"Let's see who gets there first!" I shouted to Mia as we raced to the library. My feet flew so fast that I felt like I was swimming through the air.

"Okay, but first to the swimming books!" Mia called back, grinning. We skidded to a stop in front of the 'Sports' section, breathing hard but laughing.

Swimming is my favorite—it's like being a magic fish, gliding through the water. But racing? That made my stomach do somersaults. Mia knew that and always tried to cheer me up.

I flipped through soccer and basketball books. Then, I found one and said, "Mia, look!" It had a bright cover and a swimmer's photo. The book opens with Fanny Durack's story. It made me excited. Maybe it could help with my racing worries.

It was dinner time, and I was spinning my spaghetti around my fork when I remembered the swim meet coming up in a few weeks. I wasn't too nervous; I knew I was fast. But Sam and Tess were super fast. Last year, Sam had won. He could swim like a hungry shark!

"Mom," I said, looking up from my plate.

"Can I go to swimming practice more? I need to swim faster for the meet."

"Of course, Jade," Mom smiled.

"We want you to feel ready and have fun. How often do you want to go?"

"Maybe every day after school?" I suggested, hoping it wasn't too much.

Mom nodded. "Every day? Uh.....Ok, if you said so. I'll make sure you get there, champ."

I smiled, twirling more spaghetti. "Thanks, Mom! I'm going to swim super fast this year!" I was excited. Swimming was fun, and winning was even more fun.

"Oh! I also got a book from the library about a swimmer named Fanny Durack," I added. I remembered the book with the swimmer on the cover. "I haven't read it yet. But, the back cover says she was the first female gold medalist in Olympic swimming."

"That sounds amazing," Mom said. "Maybe her story can give you some tips for your swim meet."

"Yeah! I'll start reading it tonight!" I was curious about Fanny and how she swam so well. Maybe I could learn something from her!

Fanny's Story

I was sitting on my bed, my tablet lighting up with Mia's face.

I had just started reading the book about Fanny Durack and couldn't wait to tell Mia all about it.

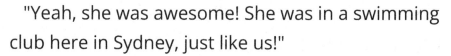

"Hey, Mia! I started reading that Fanny book," I said, my eyes wide with excitement.

"Ooh, tell me! Was she like a swimming legend?" Mia bounced a little, her face close to her camera.

"Yeah, she was awesome! She was in a swimming club here in Sydney, just like us!"

"No way! She was from Sydney, too?" Mia looked surprised.

"Yep! But even though she had a place to swim, she faced many challenges because girls weren't supposed to race back then," I continued.

"That's so unfair!" Mia frowned.

"Super unfair! But even though they told her "NO" lots of times, she didn't give up. She kept trying over and over."

"So cool! Like us not giving up on beating Sam!" Mia punched the air.

"Exactly! Fanny and her friend were the first women ever to compete in Olympic swimming from

Australia. Before them, no woman had ever swum in the Olympics!" I added, amazed by Fanny's courage.

"Whoa, that's crazy! How did she manage to go?" Mia leaned in, curious.

"She kept fighting until they let her swim. It was a huge deal," I said, feeling inspired by Fanny's determination.

"And then what happened at the Olympics?" Mia's voice was full of excitement.

"She went all the way to Stockholm for the Olympics in 1912, and guess what? She won the gold medal!" I couldn't hide my excitement.

"Gold? Like the best of the best?" Mia's eyes sparkled.

"Yeah, the very best! Incredible, right? I wish I could ask her for some advice about my swim meet!" I said.

"Well, be a Fanny Durack!" Mia cheered, and we laughed.

Jade's Inspiration

After talking to Mia, I lay on my bed with the book about Fanny Durack. Fanny was brave, swimming when no girls were supposed to. She won gold despite the difficulty. I felt nervous about the upcoming swim meet with Sam and Tess, who were so fast. What if I couldn't beat them?

But then, I remembered Fanny. She didn't quit, and neither would I. I jumped up, feeling a rush of excitement.

"I'm going to swim in the meet, and I'm going to do my best, just like Fanny!" I declared out loud to my empty room.

I was at the community center pool the next afternoon, ready to practice. My coach blew the whistle, and I dived in. The water felt cool and exciting around me. Each stroke made me feel stronger.

"Remember, Jade, focus on your form, not just speed!" Coach yelled from the side.

I nodded and kept swimming, thinking about how Fanny might have practiced, pushing through even when it was tough.

After practice, Mom picked me up and handed me a snack. "How was swimming today?" she asked, smiling.

"Good! I'm trying to swim like Fanny Durack. She never gave up," I said, munching on an apple.

"That's my girl. Keep that spirit, and you'll do great," Mom encouraged, ruffling my wet hair.

At home, Dad had put up a picture of Fanny Durack near my study table. "See, Jade? Whenever you feel tired or unsure, just look at Fanny. Remember, she swam her way to gold," he said, winking.

"Yeah, Dad! If Fanny can do it, I can at least try my best at the meet," I smiled broadly, feeling less worried about Sam and Tess.

I lay back on my bed, my heart thumping with excitement and nervousness. I've always loved swimming. Now, clutching the book about Fanny Durack, a spark ignites inside me—I don't just want to swim; I want to win.

Every day, I practiced, sometimes feeling like my arms would fall off, but I didn't stop. Fanny didn't have it easy and still swam like a champion. I would give the swim meet everything I have.

"I'm going to compete, and I want to try my best!" I whispered to myself, feeling a surge of determination.

The next day at the community center pool, I jumped in with a big splash, swimming harder than ever because I wanted to do my best!

"Jade, focus on each move you make!" Coach Abby called from the side of the pool. "Make every stroke count!"

I popped my head up, panting.

"Coach, I've always just swam for fun. But now... I really want to try to win. I want to be like Fanny," I confessed, feeling the water drip down my face.

Coach Abby walked closer, her face serious but encouraging.

"Jade, remember, winning starts in your heart and your head. It's not just about how fast you swim, but how much you believe you can do it," she explained, crouching by the pool to meet my gaze.

"But what if I'm not good enough?" The worry was nagging at me, making my stomach twist.

"Jade, you have the spirit and the strength. Trust in your training, believe in yourself, and push through no matter what happens, just like Fanny. She swam against more than water; she swam against doubt, and she never let it stop her," Coach Abby encouraged, handing me my goggles.

Taking a deep breath, I put on my goggles and nodded. "Okay, I'm going to swim my heart out," I said, feeling a new wave of courage.

Every day in the pool was a challenge. My arms ached, my breath was short, but my heart was full. I thought about Fanny and how she kept swimming even when things were tough, and it pushed me to keep going.

"Jade, it's just you and the water," Coach Abby called out as I took another lap.

"Try to make each lap a little bit better than the one before. You're getting stronger every day!"

Her words stuck with me, splashing in my mind with every stroke. As the swim meet neared, I wasn't swimming for fun anymore; I was swimming to prove something to myself.

Mom noticed my focus as I packed my swim bag the night before the meet.

"You've got a fire in you this time, Jade," she said, helping me with my gear.

"I want to make every stroke count, Mom. I want to show that I can do more," I said, zipping up my bag with determination.

Mom gave me a big hug. "You're already making us proud, Jade. Just go out there and swim your best. That's all anyone can ask for."

That night, in bed, I replayed the race in my mind. Nervous but excited, I aimed for a victory like never before. I was ready to swim with the same passion as Fanny.

The School Swim Meet

The big day of the school swim meet had arrived, and the air buzzed with excitement and nervous energy, just like an Olympic event. I stood by the pool, my heart pounding like a drum. I could see Sam smirking from the other side of the pool, looking so sure he'd win again this year. Tess was stretching, her face serious, whispering to her friends that she was the fastest.

"Jade! You got this!" I heard Mia's voice over the crowd, and I saw her waving a big, colorful sign that said, 'Go Jade!' My family was there too, cheering for me.

I remembered the book of Fanny Durack at the 1912 Olympics. She faced the world with her brave heart. I took a deep breath. "Swim your best, Jade," I whispered to myself, thinking about Fanny's courage.

The whistle blew, and we all jumped into the water. The cold splash shocked me, but I kicked harder. Sam was fast, his arms slicing through the water like a shark. Tess was right next to me, and for a moment, I saw her glance my way, her eyes fierce.

Halfway through, I turned at the wall, kicking off hard. I didn't slow down. I thought of Fanny, pushing through the water, focusing only on her race.

The cheers grew louder, and I could hear Mia's voice rising above the rest. "Come on, Jade!" she yelled. My legs felt like they were flying. Mia kept cheering, "You can do it, Jade!"

I gathered all my strength. I thought of Fanny Durack. She pushed through every hard moment. "For Fanny!" I whispered to myself. With one massive kick off the wall and a powerful pull of my arms, I surged forward like a rocket.

In the last few meters, it was just the splash of the water, the pounding of my heart, and the line at the end of the pool. Sam was just ahead, and Tess was at my side. With one final surge, I pushed with everything I had left. My hands hit the wall, and I gasped for air, turning to see the scoreboard.

I won!

The crowd erupted, and Mia screamed my name, tears of joy running down her face.

"Jade! You did it! You're the champion!" She rushed over as I climbed out of the pool, and we hugged tightly, laughing and crying.

"I can't believe it, Mia! We did it!" I said, my voice shaky with excitement and disbelief. I felt like I could conquer anything. This wasn't just a win but a moment I'd remember forever.

After the swim meet, I stood holding my shiny new medal, feeling taller and prouder than ever. I couldn't stop smiling as I thought about how hard I had swum and how loud my friends and family had cheered.

"Mia, I did it! I really did it!" I said, still amazed that I had won.

"You swam like a jet airplane, Jade!" Mia replied, her eyes sparkling with happiness.

Looking at my medal, I realized that winning wasn't just about being the fastest.

It was about trying my best, being brave, and believing in myself. It was about pushing through, even when things felt super hard. That's what made me feel proud.

A photo of Fanny Durack on the wall next to my bed. Fanny taught me that you could do anything if you set your mind to it and keep trying, no matter what. Every time I look at her picture, I remember her courage and determination.

"I'll always keep swimming towards my dreams," I thought. And with that picture on my wall, I knew I would always be inspired to swim my best, face my fears, and chase after my biggest dreams.

Jade's lesson:

Jade learned that winning is about trying her best and believing in herself, even when things are tough. She discovered that perseverance is very important, which means keeping on trying even when it is really hard. It can make her dreams come true.

Message to you from Jade:

Hi! Always believe in yourself, keep trying no matter what, and remember, you can achieve incredible things

by being brave and never giving up on your dreams!
Love, Jade

Author's Note

Hello girl,

In this book, we journey alongside Fanny Durack, a real-life hero from history who made waves by being the first woman to win a gold medal in swimming at the 1912 Olympics. I've shared some true details about her amazing achievements to inspire you!

While Fanny's dedication and triumph are real, some of the challenges and conversations in our story come from my imagination. I added these to make our adventure with Fanny even more exciting and to show what it might feel like to overcome big obstacles.

I hope this story has inspired you to learn more about Fanny and other amazing people from the past! They did some pretty awesome things, and there's so much we can learn from them.

Love, Jenny

CHAPTER 10

The Magical Window to Adventure

In class today, Mrs. Thompson brought in a new girl.

Mrs.Thompson seemed happy.

"Class, this is Gina. She's just moved here from Egypt," she said.

Gina looked at us and waved a little.

"Hello, I'm Gina," she said, but she sounded different.

"Why does she talk like that?" I whispered to my friend Coco.

Mrs. Thompson heard me.

"Ameria, everyone's voice is unique. Let's welcome Gina warmly," she said.

Later, we had to do a group project. I watched Gina. She worked with Jack, but they didn't talk much. Their project didn't look fun. Coco leaned over to me, giggling.

"Looks like Jack and Gina aren't having much fun, huh?"

"Yeah, they're so quiet!" I giggled back.

"Ameria and Gina, you'll work together next on a world history project," Mrs. Thompson said. "Remember, everyone gets a different partner, class!"

"But Mrs. Thompson, can I please work with Coco?" I asked quickly. "We always do good projects together. Plus, we're best friends."

Mrs. Thompson shook her head gently. "I think it's a great chance to make a new friend and learn something new, Ameria."

"But what if it's like Jack's project? It wasn't very good," I said, now really worried.

Mrs. Thompson smiled.

"It's all about trying, Ameria. You and Gina can do great if you share your ideas openly."

I wasn't sure about this at all.

Ameria's Everyday

I love being with my friends at school. We all talk and laugh a lot. Everyone here speaks English, just like me. It's easy because we all understand everything.

This morning, I was talking with my friends about our weekends. It was fun, and I felt happy.

"Guess what? I got a new puppy!" Coco said looking like she was jumping and dancing.

"Really? What's its name?" I asked, my eyes wide with curiosity.

"It's Fluffy!" Coco laughed, and everyone else giggled.

Then, Mrs. Thompson asked us in class, "Can anyone tell me why we speak English here?"

I knew the answer! "Because it's the best language, and everyone understands it!" I said.

Mrs. Thompson smiled. "Well, English is one of many languages spoken around the world. Each language is important to its speakers."

Jake chimed in, "My grandma speaks Spanish. She taught me to say 'te quiero mucho!'"

"What does that mean?" I asked, puzzled because I didn't understand those words.

"It means 'I love you a lot!' in Spanish," Jake explained.

"Oh," I said, a bit surprised. I never thought about how words could be different in other languages. It sounded strange, not like the everyday words we use.

That was a new idea, but soon, we did some reading and math, and I didn't think about it much more. I was sure everyone should speak English—it's much easier.

School is my favorite place because it's just like me. But when Gina came, I wasn't quite sure if I wanted things to change.

The School Diversity Celebration Project

Mrs. Thompson announced our next project in class today. "We're going to learn about world history," she said with a big smile.

"Everyone, please find your assigned partners and sit together," Mrs. Thompson instructed with a smile.

"But why?" I whispered to Coco before turning back to look at Gina, who was already walking towards me.

"Hi, Ameria! I'm excited to work with you!" Gina said, smiling big. I didn't smile back. I was worried. What if her different way of seeing things made our project weird?

Mrs. Thompson must have noticed my frown.

"Ameria, Gina knows a lot about Egypt's history. I think you can learn something special from her," she encouraged me.

Gina started talking about pyramids and pharaohs.

"Did you know that the pyramids were built by thousands of workers over many years?" she asked.

I nodded, even though I didn't know that.

"But how does that help us with our project?" I asked.

"It shows how people can work together to create something amazing," Gina explained.

I still wasn't sure.

"But it's so old. What does that have to do with us now?" I asked.

Gina laughed a little. History helps us understand how people lived. It shows what they thought was important. It's like a story that happened!"

Mrs. Thompson came over. "See, Ameria? Learning from each other can make your project even better."

I listened, but I still wasn't sure. Gina's ideas were so different. Could this really work? I guess I had to find out.

Jumping Back in Time

Gina pulled a gold-covered book from the library shelf, her eyes wide with excitement.

"Ameria, look! It says it's about time travel."

"Really?" I peeked over her shoulder, unsure. We sat cross-legged on the floor, the old book opened between us.

"Is it okay to read this out loud?"

Gina nodded eagerly. "Let's find out what it says!"

We began reading together, and as we did, a shimmer started swirling around us.

"Gina, what's that?" I pointed, my voice shaky.

"It's a portal, Ameria! It's really working!" Gina clapped her hands.

"A portal? Like, a real one?" I couldn't believe it. My heart raced.

"Yes! We could see ancient Egypt—think of what I could show you about where I'm from, but a long time ago!" Gina's eyes sparkled with the thrill of sharing her heritage.

"But what if something happens to us there?" My thoughts raced with all the things that could go wrong.

Gina squeezed my hand.

"We'll be fine. We'll see the pyramids and meet pharaohs!"

I hesitated, watching the light dance faster. "Are we really doing this?"

Gina smiled broadly, pulling me to my feet. "On three—one, two, three!"

Together, we walked into a bright light. It felt unique, warm, and tingly. As it faded, we found ourselves in a lively market. There, we heard merchants and smelled spices.

"We did it! We're in Egypt!" Gina's laughter filled the air.

I looked around, amazed. "It's like we're in a history book come to life!"

"Exactly! Think of all we can learn here!" Gina was already pulling me towards a stall of colorful fabrics.

"Wait, look at that!" I pointed at a group of children playing with a ball made of rags. "They play games just like us!"

"Everything's so different, yet some things are the same," Gina observed, her eyes taking in every detail.

"Maybe this wasn't such a crazy idea," I admitted, a smile spreading as my fear faded.

"First stop, the palace! Maybe we'll meet Cleopatra!" Gina tugged at my hand, and together, we dove deeper into the heart of ancient Egypt, ready for whatever lay ahead.

Meeting Cleopatra and Learning from the Past

As we walked through the grand corridors of Cleopatra's palace, the air was thick with the scent of incense and the murmur of distant conversations. Finally, we reached a room where Queen Cleopatra sat gracefully on her throne.

"Who are these young visitors that time has brought to my court?" Cleopatra's voice echoed softly through the grand space.

Gina stepped forward, speaking clearly.

"Your Majesty, we come from the future. In our time, you are celebrated as a great leader."

"From the future, you say? And what wisdom do you seek in the past?" Cleopatra asked, her eyes curious.

"We're learning about leadership and how to understand people who are different from us," I chimed in, trying to sound confident.

"A wise endeavor," Cleopatra nodded. "Understanding different perspectives is crucial for any leader. Do you practice this in your time?"

I hesitated, then admitted, "Not really, I haven't tried much."

Gina gave me a small nudge, "That's why we're here, to learn."

Cleopatra smiled and stood up.

"Come with me. Let me show you the importance of seeing the world through many eyes."

She led us to a balcony that overlooked the bustling city.

"Behold my city—here, people from various lands bring their goods and their stories. All are welcome, and all are valued."

"How do you ensure everyone feels welcome?" I asked, watching the crowd below.

"With respect and curiosity," Cleopatra explained. "Respecting someone means recognizing their worth. Being curious about them means you are open to learning from them."

"That's something I need to work on," I said, thinking about Gina and how I first reacted to her.

"And what about happiness? How do you make sure everyone is happy?" I asked, wanting to know how she did it.

"Happiness comes from feeling understood and valued. It is not just about cooperation but about genuine connection and respect," Cleopatra explained. She then gestured for us to follow her deeper into the palace.

As we walked, she showed us pictures on the wall of people from different places being friends.

"Each of these grand paintings represents how we, like true friends from different lands, share respect and joy, not just for our benefit, but for our happiness together."

"Wow, so they're like special friends from all over the world!" Ameria said, amazed at how friendly they looked.

We stopped by a stall where a merchant was selling spices from faraway lands.

"This merchant brings spices from India. Such trades bring us more than goods—they bring knowledge and create happiness through shared prosperity," she explained.

"It's like when we share our ideas in school projects," I said, smiling as I started to understand.

"Exactly," Cleopatra agreed. "Sharing ideas is a powerful way to build understanding and happiness."

We continued our tour, and Cleopatra showed us a garden where people from different cultures were talking and laughing together.

"See how they share their stories? This is how happiness and cooperation grow. They learn from each other, and their respect for each other deepens."

"Understanding different ideas really helps you think better," I said as it started making sense to me.

As the sun dipped below the horizon, the portal flickered to life once more.

"It is time for your return. May these lessons guide you both," Cleopatra said, her voice soft but firm.

"Thank you for everything," Gina said, her voice thick with emotion.

"I've learned so much about accepting others and about happiness," I added. "I'll try to be more open and listen to different ideas."

"You will be a great leader one day," Cleopatra assured us with a warm smile.

Stepping back through the portal, we returned to the library. The world hadn't changed, but we had.

"Was that real? Did we really just meet Cleopatra?" I asked Gina, my eyes wide as I looked around the familiar library, half-expecting it to have transformed.

"I think so... It felt real!" Gina replied, touching the books on the shelf to ensure she was back in reality.

"Can you believe we just met Cleopatra?" I continued, still trying to wrap my head around the adventure.

"I know! And she taught us so much!" Gina replied, her voice filled with wonder and a bit of disbelief.

"We were standing right there, learning about history from someone who made it!"

"It's incredible, isn't it? We have to include all of this in our project!" Gina suggested eagerly.

"It'll be the best one yet!" I agreed. My doubts gave way to a new enthusiasm for sharing what we'd learned.

As we left the library, the outside world seemed bigger. It was filled with endless possibilities. I felt ready to explore them. I now understand what it means to connect with others. I saw how it creates happiness. You do it through respect and cooperation.

Sharing Their Journey

"Okay, so how do we start our presentation?" I asked Gina, spreading out all our notes and pictures across the library table.

Gina laughed, arranging some pretend 'artifacts' we had made.

"Let's open with, 'Last weekend, we took a little trip... back to ancient Egypt!'"

I giggled, imagining our classmates' faces.

"Yes! And we can show them this 'ancient' scroll we brought back," I said, holding up a piece of paper we had coffee-stained to look old.

"As Cleopatra says..." Gina began in a dramatic voice, draping a fabric like a toga around her shoulders.

I joined in, trying not to laugh, "To lead is to understand, and to understand is to explore!'"

We spent the rest of the afternoon improving our presentation. We used our story to showcase Egypt's rich history and culture. We couldn't wait to show everyone how much fun learning can be.

The Class History Project

"Hey, everyone, let's come together for our history project presentation!" I called out cheerfully as everyone started to gether around.

"Today, we're taking you back to ancient Egypt, and guess what? We met Cleopatra!" Gina started; her eyes wide with excitement.

"We did! And Cleopatra taught us how to make the best Egyptian flatbread!" I chimed in, holding up a plate of flatbread we had made.

"Did you know Cleopatra was super smart? She spoke many languages and was friends with people from all over the world," I added, spreading out a map to show all the places.

"Yeah, and she told us that being friends with people from different places made her a better queen," Gina continued.

"Because when you understand people from different places, you can do better together!" I explained, pointing to pictures of Cleopatra and other leaders.

"Now, who's got questions about our adventure or Cleopatra?" Gina asked, scanning the eager faces.

"Did Cleopatra have a favorite food?" one classmate asked curiously.

"Actually, yes! She loved figs and honey, but not sure about favorite." I answered, remembering our 'research.'

"Did she have a pet?" another hand shot up.

"Maybe! There is no evidence, but Egyptians loved cats," Gina smiled.

"What was the coolest thing you learned from her?" another classmate asked.

We looked at each other, and I said, "That being curious about others is important. It makes the world a friendlier place!" I concluded, feeling proud of our presentation.

Our classmates clapped, and some even said they wanted to learn more about other countries. Our history project turned out to be not just a lesson but a hit show full of fun and giggles. Everyone learned a lot and had a great time doing it!

Ameria's New World View

"Hey Gina, can you believe I used to think America was the best, and that was it?" I said, looking up from my notebook.

Gina giggled, "Really? That's funny, Ameria! But now you know there's a whole world out there, right?"

"Yeah, now I see it. America is cool, but it's just one place. Other places are awesome, too!" I scribbled more in my notebook, excited about this new idea.

"It's great you're seeing how every culture has something special," Gina nodded. "It's like having a world party, and everyone's invited!"

"That's exactly it! I want to learn about everyone and share it. It makes us all better friends," I added, feeling happy about how much I'd changed.

Classroom Changes

The next day in class, I stood up, feeling a bit nervous but excited.

"Everyone, let's start a 'Culture Club.' Each week, someone can share something cool about where they're from or where they want to go!"

"That sounds amazing, Ameria! I'll bring pictures from Vietnam next week," Linh called out from her desk.

"Our class is like a mini world tour!" Mrs. Thompson said, clapping her hands.

"Ameria and Gina, thank you for bringing us closer with your stories and ideas."

Everyone cheered, and I felt super happy. It was like our classroom had become a new and exciting place where everyone could be themselves and share their stories.

I wanted to know more about everyone's stories.

"Hey Miguel, what's something awesome about Mexico?" I asked, eager to keep the cultural exchange going.

"Have you ever heard of piñatas? We make these colorful, paper-mâché creations you break for celebrations," Miguel explained, his eyes lighting up.

"Piñatas? Are they from Mexico?" I laughed.

"You have to show me how to make one!"

As we talked, more classmates joined in. Soon, we were sharing stories from Vietnam and Nigeria.

Seeing our excitement, Mrs. Thompson suggested, "Why not make every month a journey to a new country right here at school?"

"Like a trip around the world without leaving the classroom?" I said, thrilled at the idea.

"Yes, exactly!" Mrs. Thompson smiled. "We can explore new foods, music, and art. It'll be our global tour."

The idea took off. We planned a Vietnamese food day, an African music workshop, and an art day inspired by famous painters from around the world.

"Who knew learning about history and cultures could be this much fun?" I said to Gina.

"Right? I think Cleopatra would be proud of us for making our school such a cool place to learn about each other," Gina replied, her eyes twinkling.

As we talked, the possibilities seemed endless. We had the whole world to explore and so many stories to discover. And I knew that with each adventure, I'd learn something new about the world and myself.

Ameria's Lesson:

Ameria found out that learning about different cultures makes school more fun! It also helps her understand her friends better. She loves learning what makes each place so cool and unique, and seeing how everyone has something great to share.

Message to you from Ameria:

"Hi! Start your own adventure by learning about other places and people. You'll make so many new friends and have so much fun! Let's explore the world together!" Love, Ameria

Dear Families and Friends,

Thank you for joining us on this adventure with your wonderful girl! We hope our stories have touched her heart and become a special part of your bedtime routine. We'd love to hear about it!

Your feedback not only supports our work but also helps bring these stories to more families like yours. We would be truly grateful if you could take a moment to leave a review!

Simply scan this QR code with your phone.
Alternative way: Follow the steps below to leave a review on Amazon.

    1. Visit the book's page on Amazon

    2. Scroll down to "Write a Customer Review."

    3. Rate us with stars, or share a few words
       about your favorite story!

Thank you so much for your invaluable support!
Love, Jenny

Word Bank

Anxious (ad.): Feeling worried or nervous. *Example: She felt anxious before her big test at school.*

Astonishment (noun): A big surprise that makes you feel amazed or shocked. *Example: Her face showed astonishment when she saw the giant birthday cake.*

Beacon (noun): A light or something that guides people. *Example: The lighthouse was a beacon for the ships.*

Brave (adj.): Showing no fear of dangerous or difficult things. *Example: She was brave to speak in front of the whole class.*

Confidence (noun): Feeling sure about what you can do. *Example: He spoke with confidence about his art project.*

Concern (noun): A worry about something important. *Example: His main concern was getting home before dark.*

Courage (noun): Being brave and doing something even though it is scary or hard. *Example: It takes courage to stand up to bullies. It took a lot of courage for her to stand up in front of the class and tell her story.*

Crucial (adj.): Very important. *Example: Finding your homework is crucial for school tomorrow.*

Curiosity (noun): Wanting to learn or know about something. *Example: Her curiosity made her read all about planets.*

Determination (noun): Not giving up, even when things are tough. *Example: His determination helped him finish the race.*

Diverse (adj.): Different from each other. *Example: Our class is diverse, with students from many countries.*

Doubt (noun): Not being certain. *Example: She had doubts about which ice cream to choose.*

Eager (adj.): Really wanting to do or see something. *Example: He was eager to open his birthday gifts.*

Embrace (verb): To accept something happily. *Example: She embraced her new role as a big sister.*

Empathy (noun): Understanding how someone else feels. *Example: She showed empathy by comforting her friend.*

Empower (verb): To give someone strength or confidence. *Example: The teacher's kind words empowered the students.*

Endeavor (noun): A big effort to do something. *Example: The science project was a big endeavor for the class.*

Enthusiasm (noun): Being very excited about something. *Example: He showed his enthusiasm by clapping loudly.*

Frightening (adj.): Making you feel scared. *Example: The loud thunder was frightening.*

Glanced (verb): To quickly look at something. *Example: She glanced at the clock during the test.*

Grateful (adj.): Feeling thankful. *Example: He was grateful for the homemade cookies.*

Grin (verb): To smile widely. *Example: She couldn't stop grinning when she got a pet kitten.*

Heritage (noun): The history and culture that come from a family's past. *Example: We learned about our family's heritage.*

Huddle (verb): To come close together in a group. *Example: The team huddled together to make a plan.*

Imigongo (noun): A type of colorful art from Rwanda made from cow dung. *Example: They looked at the beautiful Imigongo at the museum.*

Inner strength (noun): Personal power and courage inside you. *Example: His inner strength helped him deal with tough times.*

Inspire (verb): To make someone feel that they can do something good. *Example: Her coach's words inspire her to improve.*

Mumble (verb): To speak quietly and unclearly. *Example: He mumbled his answer so I couldn't hear.*

Mutter (verb): To speak softly and usually in a negative way. *Example: She muttered a complaint under her breath.*

Overcome (verb): To succeed in dealing with a problem. *Example: She overcame her fear of heights by climbing a ladder.*

Perseverance (noun): Keep trying, even when something is difficult. *Example: Her perseverance was clear when she finished the race, even though she was tired.*

Perspective (noun): A way of thinking about something. *Example: She had a different perspective and liked the new song.*

Resilience (noun): *Bouncing back quickly from tough times. Example: Even after falling off her bike, she showed resilience by getting right back on and trying again.*

Setback (noun): *A problem that makes things a little or a lot harder. Example: The rain was a setback for our picnic, but we had it inside instead.*

Shrugged (verb): To lift your shoulders up and down to show you don't know or care. *Example: He shrugged when asked about his homework.*

Trotting (verb): To run at a speed that is slower than a gallop but faster than walking. Example: *The puppy was trotting along the path, happy to be outside.*

Unmistakable (adj.): Very clear; impossible to confuse with something else. *Example: The smell of cookies was unmistakable.*

Vigorously (adv.): Doing something with a lot of energy and strength. *Example: She vigorously shook the bottle to mix the juice.*

Made in the USA
Las Vegas, NV
26 November 2024

12682330R00098